Better Spelling In 30 Minutes a Day

By
Robert W. Emery and Harry H. Crosby

CAREER PRESS
3 Tice Road
P.O. Box 687
Franklin Lakes, NJ 07417
1-800-CAREER-1
201-848-0310 (outside U.S.)
FAX: 201-848-1727

BETTER SPELLING IN 30 MINUTES A DAY
Cover design by The Visual Group
Printed in the U.S.A. by Book-mart Press

To order this title, please call toll-free 1-800-CAREER-1
(NJ and Canada: 201-848-0310) to order using VISA or
MasterCard, or for further information on books from
Career Press.

Library of Congress Cataloging-in-Publication Data

Emery, Robert W.
    Better spelling in 30 minutes a day / by Robert W. Emery and Harry
H. Crosby.
        p.   cm.
    Includes index.
    ISBN 1-56414-202-7 (pbk.)
    1. English language—Orthography and spelling. I. Crosby, Harry
H. II. Title.
PE1145.2.E44   1995
428.1—dc20
                                              95-4818
                                              CIP

Contents

Better Spelling

Chapter 1

Diagnostics

Please consider the following questions: Do you think you are a good speller? Do you frequently ask your roomate how to spell words? Do you use the dictionary more then you think you should? Have you recieved alot of low grades on your papers because of poor spelling?

What we wanted you to "consider" in the questions was the spelling. Did you notice that some words were misspelled? Look again. What are the misspelled words?

The misspelled words are *roomate* (should be *roommate*); *then* (instead of *than*); *alot,* which should be two words *(a lot)* rather than one; and *recieve* (should be *receive*).

If you were fooled by our trick and did not notice the misspelled words, you need this book. Even if you noted the misspellings, you must have some reason for having this book in your hands. Perhaps you have had evidence in the past that you do not spell well. It may be that your teachers have told you that your writing is marred by poor spelling.

● ●

1.1 The Importance of Spelling

● ●

What if you do not spell well? What if your college papers come back with misspellings circled? Why do you need to improve your spelling skills? The answer is, purely and simply, that because of the misspelling you usually get a lower grade. Time after time college teachers of all subjects have indicated that they are affected adversely by misspelling. Misspelling casts a "reverse halo" on a paper. Some college teachers seem to feel that a student who cannot spell or take the care to spell correctly has nothing important to say and deserves a poor grade.

Is this problem limited to college?

Anyone who has ever served on a search committee (a group of people whose task is to hire someone) knows the importance of the ability to spell. When a committee is appointed to hire a new director for an art center, an administrative assistant for the mayor, a new division head in a factory, or a coach of a football team, each member of the committee reads the application letters and passes them on to the next member. By the time the letters get to a third reader, any misspellings will have been circled. When the search committee looks at the first hundred or so applications, they are looking for an excuse to reject candidates. Apparently there is no easier method than to indicate misspellings, and candidates whose letters contain even one misspelling often do not get past the first round.

Are we saying that your attempts to get good grades in college and a good job afterward are jeopardized by an inability to spell?

We are. The same holds true, unfortunately, in almost any branch of human endeavor. A study at a large corporation showed that a person might get a job because of an initial skill, but to move up the ladder or to move laterally into a different department he or she needs the ability to write—and spelling is one of the most noticeable features of good writing.

All too often, spelling does keep a person from getting a good grade, from selling something, from getting a job, or from being accepted to a graduate school. It is for these reasons that this spelling textbook has been written.

1.2 Programmed Instruction

Have you used a programmed textbook before?

You may have noticed that much of what you have just read was in the form of questions and answers. This was to prepare you for the rest of the book, much of which is programmed instruction. A programmed text teaches by involving the student in a series of questions and answers. When you see a question followed by a write-in line, you should put a card or a piece of paper over the section below the line. By hiding the answers to questions, you will have an opportunity to think out an answer before you read on.

Programmed texts are useful because research shows that students understand and remember best when they get involved in a conversation. Programmed instruction also makes frequent review possible, and it helps students to skip instruction that they already know. Most importantly, it takes advantage of a crucial lesson in learning theory: There is no learning without verbalization. To remember, you must put the material into your own words; you must run it verbally through your mind. Programmed instruction, which forces the student to put into words and practice what is being learned, helps not only in learning but also in remembering.

Students using the approach described in this book have learned to spell well, and you can be one of them. Many people do not write letters; they hesitate to write memos; they will not become the secretary of a committee—all because they are not confident about their spelling. If you really give this book a try, you will develop confidence in an important part of writing. You may even be helped in a broader sense. Because you learn to be careful about details when you spell, you probably will

---

3

learn to be careful about other important details, whether in your writing or in other projects that you undertake in life.

1.3 Diagnosis

This book is based on two premises:

1. Everyone can be a good speller.
2. There is no one method of learning to spell that works for everyone.

English is indeed a language for which spelling is comparatively difficult. If you were Spanish, you would have much less trouble spelling in Spanish because all sounds are exactly represented by letters. You must not forget, however, that every year thousands and thousands of people master the problem and become good spellers. You can become one of them.

In the past you may have been subjected to instruction about how to spell. The difference between that instruction and the spelling manual that you are now reading stems from the second premise just listed: that there is no one method that works for everyone. First, you must come to "know thyself," which, as Socrates insisted, is the beginning of wisdom. You must learn what system works for you. If you have trouble spelling, your trouble may be caused by one or several reasons, and it will be your job to diagnose which reasons apply to you. This book will help.

We exposed you to the misspelling of *roommate, a lot, than and receive* in order to get you started on your self-diagnosis. If you did not catch the misspelling, do you know why? Do you not know how to spell the words, or did you just not notice? Did you say to yourself, "Oh, I was just careless"? If so, you may have "eye memory trouble." When you learned the correct spelling, did you say the words softly to yourself—*room-mate,*

4

making sure that you sounded out the two syllables? If so, you may have an "ear memory." Or did you try writing the word out, either actually with pen or pencil or in your mind? If so, you may have a "muscle memory."

As you work in this book, you will be discovering what kind of a memory you have: an eye memory, an ear memory, a muscle memory, or a logical memory. You will find that the more of these senses you have the habit of using, the more quickly and effectively you will become a good speller.

Your first task will be to get some idea of what kind of mistakes you make and how often you make them. Take the following diagnostic exercises now, and analyze your work afterward.

Spelling Diagnostic Exercises

The purpose of these exercises is not only to determine how good a speller you are, but also to help you see what kinds of spelling errors you make and therefore what you must do to remedy your troubles. Check your answers to each exercise with the answer key on pages 12-15 before proceeding to the next exercise.

Exercise 1.1

In this exercise, circle "a" or "b" to indicate whether the first or second choice is the correct spelling.

Example: ⓐ b   The test is *too / two* long.

1. a   b   Sports on television give everyone *incentitive / incentive* to participate in a healthier life.

2. a   b   It is *extreamly / extremely* doubtful that electronic media will replace books.

Better Spelling

✗ 3. (a) b Automobile *companies/companys* have been successful with cars run by wind.

✗ 4. a (b) The world now *posesses/possesses* a great natural fuel that it is ignoring.

5. a b What is dreamed of today may be a reality *tommorrow/tomorrow*.

6. a b Most *teammates/teamates* are content merely to endure each other.

7. a b Computer technology will eventually replace books and cause national *illiteracy/iliteracy*.

8. a b Religion and literature have become similar in the *past/passed* few years.

9. a b The first idea that *ocured/occurred* to me was that this was the end of the world.

10. a b Gas shortages and pollution will *therefore/therefor* become more common.

11. a b Most students do not know that we are *makeing/making* a mountain out of a molehill.

12. a b When the *reciever/receiver* is placed on the hook, the conversation ends—fortunately.

✗ 13. (a) b Television has had a bad *effect/affect* on the importance of the written word.

14. a b Everything some *athletes/atheletes* do, even if it is illegal or immoral, is approved by the most avid fans.

15. a b Oil companies will have to shift *their/they're* business to solar energy.

16. a b̲ The telephone is still *prefered/preferred* to the personal letter.

17. a b People enjoy movies on many different *occassions/occasions,* but they usually go for relaxation.

18. a b̲ *Todays/Today's* films are not always an art form.

19. a b̲ Is the newspaper *becomming/becoming* obsolete? I think so.

✗ 20. (a̲) b̲ In the newspaper you can get the complete story from *beginning/begining* to end.

21. a b The dangers of atomic energy are awesome to *ecologicaly/ecologically* minded people.

22. a̲ b *There/Their* are among both conservationists and business people some radical thinkers.

23. a b̲ Opponents must not *critisize/criticize* each other if they are to settle the problem.

✗ 24. a̲ (b̲) Plans are already beginning to *develope/develop* that have the best features from both camps.

25. a̲ b Before the candidates go *further/farther* into their discussion, they should attempt to reconcile their differences.

Better Spelling

Exercise 1.2

In the blank space write the letter indicating the misspelled word. If there is no word spelled incorrectly, leave the space blank.

Example: _C_ (a) too (b) again (c) nite (d) leaf

X 1. _C_ (a) amoung (b) loneliness (c) losing (d) grammar

2. _C_ (a) conscious (b) prejudice (c) discribe (d) controversy

X 3. ____ (a) persue (b) government (c) criticism (d) equipped

4. ____ (a) business (b) experience (c) choose (d) exist

5. _B_ (a) appear (b) surprize (c) excellent (d) argument

6. _D_ (a) rhythm (b) decision (c) analyze (d) reciept

7. _A_ (a) posess (b) embarrass (c) conscience (d) acquire

X 8. _C_ (a) controlled (b) probably (c) conscience (d) practicle

X 9. ____ (a) comparative (b) consistent (c) priviledge (d) forty

X 10. _B_ (a) exaggerate (b) imagination (c) aquaint (d) definitely

11. _A_ (a) perfessor (b) succeed (c) similar (d) shining

X 12. ____ (a) similiar (b) procedure (c) prominent (d) repetition

13. _A_ (a) begining (b) prevalent (c) referring (d) height

14. _A_ (a) who'se (b) accommodate (c) weird (d) disastrous

15. _A_ (a) worshiped (b) suppress (c) propaganda (d) ninety

16. _C_ (a) together (b) totally (c) hindrence (d) adolescence

17. _A_ (a) abundence (b) commission (c) fundamental (d) roommate

18. _D_ (a) possesses (b) equality (c) enemies (d) goverment

8

19. ___ (a) operate (b) price (c) opinion (d) opportunity

20. _D_ (a) permanent (b) liveliness (c) altogether
(d) curiculum

✗ 21. ___ (a) vacuum (b) delt (c) maintenance (d) technique

✗ 22. _A_ (a) fulfill (b) apparatus (c) cemetery (d) warrent

23. _A_ (a) tradgedy (b) tomorrow (c) lives (d) heroine

24. _C_ (a) perceive (b) believe (c) foriegn (d) retrieve

✗ 25. ___ (a) predjudice (b) grammar (c) persistent
(d) referring

Exercise 1.3

In the blank space write only the letters indicating the correctly spelled words. Some spaces may be left blank; in some cases you need to fill in more than one letter. Your task is to indicate which words are spelled correctly.

Example: _C_ (a) realy (b) truely (c) absolutely (d) organicly

✗ 1. _ACD_ (a) absence (b) changable (c) enviroment
(d) immediatly

✗ 2. _A_ (a) acceptance (b) changeing (c) equiptment
(d) ignorence

✗ 3. _B_ (a) acommodate (b) choose (c) excape (d) guarentee

4. _AB_ (a) analyze (b) alcohol (c) appearence (d) definate

✗ 5. _BCD_ (a) defendent (b) courteous (c) sophomore
(d) hypocrisy

✗ 6. _ABC_ (a) library (b) professor (c) really (d) vengance

7. _ABCD_ (a) fourteen (b) forty (c) ninth (d) ninety

✗ 8. _AC_ (a) surprise (b) primative (c) probably (d) unnecesary

---

9

Better Spelling

✗ 9. _A D_ (a) prominent (b) maintenence (c) irrelevent (d) syllable

✗ 10 _A B D_ (a) audience (b) dilemma (c) hypocracy (d) dominant

✗ 11. _B C_ (a) alright (b) embarrass (c) foreign (d) gost

✗ 12. _C D_ (a) discribe (b) dissappearance (c) hurriedly (d) dependent

✗ 13. _C D_ (a) calender (b) cemetary (c) benefited (d) height

✗ 14. _B_ (a) guidence (b) heroes (c) elligible (d) pronounciation

✗ 15. _____ (a) interupt (b) inventer (c) mathmatics (d) medecine

✗ 16. _____ (a) iresistible (b) irresistable (c) persistant (d) ommitted

✗ 17. _____ (a) reccommend (b) releave (c) relligion (d) sargeant

✗ 18. _a_ (a) misuse (b) rescheduleing (c) coperate (d) arrangment

✗ 19. _B C_ (a) inteligent (b) permanent (c) singling (d) trafic

✗ 20. _D_ (a) wierd (b) verticle (c) vilain (d) writing

✗ 21. _B_ (a) persue (b) license (c) naturaly (d) reccommend

✗ 22. _____ (a) proffessor (b) personell (c) procede (d) publickly

23. _C_ (a) quanity (b) grusome (c) humorous (d) exagerated

✗ 24. _D_ (a) tradgedy (b) niether (c) succede (d) inoculate

25. _A B C_ (a) discipline (b) eighth (c) employee (d) vacume

---

Exercise 1.4

This rather ridiculous paragraph is part of a slightly edited advertisement for a series of books that taught young people of the 1920s how to develop manners and social graces. You are to proofread this paragraph, find the misspelled words, and spell

them correctly in the left margin. There may be some lines with
no errors.

A Tuna Fish Sandwich Again!

1. *Already* By her third date with him, she was allready

2. *effect* in love. Concerned about its affect on him,

3. *achieve* she wore her best frock, hoping to acheive

✗ 4. _____ the impression that she was never embarased.
She wanted to fascinate him or at

5. _____ least make him like her, at least just a little.

6. _____ Across the table at the restaurant from him

7. *benefit* she saw him smile at her. She felt the benifit of
his confidence. She smiles back self-

✗ 8. *consciencely* consciencely at him. What wonderful,

9. *noticeable* noticable poise he has! What complete

10. *self-possession* self-posession! If only she could be so

✗ 11. *thouroughly* thouroughly at ease!

12. *their* Now, the most embarrassing part of there

13. *exaggerated* evening. Her fears are exagerated; now she

14. *foreign* must order from the menu of foriegn foods.

15. *than* She hopes she will perform better then last time.

✗ 16. *prominent* The waiter approaches. He has a prominant

17. *definitely* nose, and he definately is trying to scare her,

✗ 18. *succeede* and he knows he will succede. She looks at the
menu. She frowns. Now that she

✗ 19. *dineing* is dinning out, she knows she should

20. _____ order something fancy. She hears

11

21. _____ her voice saying "A tuna fish

22. _Horrified_ sandwich, please." Horofied she thinks, "He will think I can't order."

23. _occasion_ It was on that ocassion that Amelia

24. _occurred_ made a decision. Since this had occured

25. _too_ to many times before, she decided to buy that famous book, *How to Be Successful with the Opposite Sex.*

Diagnostic Exercises Answer Key

	Answer	Category
Exercise 1.1	1. b	7
	2. b	6
	3. a	3
	4. b	6
	5. b	6
	6. a	6
	7. a	5
	8. a	4
	9. b	3
	10. a	7
	11. b	5
	12. b	3
	13. a	4
	14. a	6
	15. a	4
	16. b	3
	17. b	6
	18. b	5
	19. b	3
	20. a	3

	Answer	Category
	21. b	5
	22. a	4
	23. b	7
	24. b	7
	25. a	4
Exercise 1.2	1. a	6,7
	2. c	6
	3. a	6,7
	4. no error	
	5. b	6,7
	6. d	3
	7. a	6
	8. d	6
	9. c	6,7
	10. c	6
	11. a	6
	12. a	6
	13. a	3
	14. a	5
	15. no error	
	16. c	5
	17. a	5
	18. d	6
	19. no error	
	20. d	6
	21. b	7
	22. d	6
	23. a	6,7
	24. c	3
	25. a	6,7

Better Spelling

	Answer	Category
Exercise 1.3	1. a, c, d	6
	2. a	5,6
	3. b	6,7
	4. a,b	6,7
	5. b,c,d	6,7
	6. a,b,c	6,7,5
	7. a,b,c,d	6,7
	8. a,c	6,7,5
	9. a,d	6,5
	10. a,b,d	6,5
	11. b,c	6,3
	12. c,d	5
	13. c,d	6,5,3
	14. b	6,7
	15. none	6
	16. none	6
	17. none	3,6,7
	18. a	6,5
	19. b,c	5,6
	20. d	5,7
	21. b	6,7
	22. none	6,4
	23. c	6
	24. d	3,5
	25. a,b,c	6
Exercise 1.4	1. already	4
	2. effect	4
	3. achieve	3
	4. embarrassed	6
	5. none	6
	6. none	6

1.3 Diagnosis

Answer	Category
7. benefit	6
8. self-consciously	6
9. noticeable	5
10. self-possession	6
11. thoroughly	6,7
12. their	4
13. exaggerated	6
14. foreign	3
15. than	4
16. prominent	6
17. definitely	6,7
18. succeed	6
19. dining	3
20. none	
21. none	
22. Horrified	6,7
23. occasion	6
24. occurred	3
25. too	4

Interpretation of the Diagnostic Test

Using the answer key, find out how many mistakes you made. You must have the answer completely correct to get credit for it. If there were to be two answers, for instance, you must have both answers. Subtract the number of your errors from 100 and enter the result at "Number of answers correct" on the Spelling Profile.

Spelling Profile

1. _59_ Number of answers correct   _41_

2. _____ Percentile   _____

                                             Number of Errors

3. _____ Category 3   _____
   (violation of spelling rules)

4. _____ Category 4   _____
   (words often confused)

5. _____ Category 5   _____
   (beginnings, endings, and apostrophes)

6. _____ Category 6   _____
   (phonics, pronunciations)

7. _____ Category 7   _____
   (words that won't stay put, inconsistent words, outlaws)

You can then determine how you compare to other spellers by checking the chart "Percentile Ranking of Spellers." In the left column find the number of blanks that you filled in correctly. In the corresponding right column you can find your percentile, which is your rank among approximately five hundred students who took the test. The test group was average for a typical college or university freshman class. If you scored 74, your percentile is 51, which means that 51 percent of the tested students scored below you. You are therefore about in the middle of the test group.

When you determine your percentile, enter it on the Spelling Profile.

Percentile Ranking of Spellers

Number Correct	Percentile	Number Correct	Percentile
88 or above	99	72	45
86-87	95	71	43
85	91	70	39
84	89	69	33
83	85	68	31
82	83	67	21
81	79	66	20
80	77	65	19
79	69	64	17
78	65	63	15
77	63	62	11
76	59	61	9
75	55	60	5
74	51	59	③
73	47	58 or below	1

Your next step is to determine what kinds of mistakes you made and thus decide on which sections of the book you should spend the most time and effort. Look at your examination and count the number of mistakes you made in Category 3; enter this number in the appropriate slot under "Number of Errors." Category 3 tells you whether you seem to understand certain basic spelling rules. If you missed more than five Category 3 words, put a check in the blank at 3. This means that you should emphasize your study of Chapter 3, a review of spelling rules.

Now count the number of words indicated as Category 4, and put that number below "Number of Errors." If you missed more than four in this category, put a check mark before the 4. This means that you will need to work on Chapter 4, which will help you spell correctly words that are often confused with other words.

Now repeat the process for the other categories. Check those categories that exceed these numbers:

Category	Number of Errors
3	5
4	4
5	8
6	10
7	5

These numbers indicate that, in comparison to the tested group, anyone doing less well than the above scores would be in the bottom two-thirds of the group—and we assume that you want to be better than that. You should first complete the next chapter on how to improve your proofreading. Then look at your profile and plan to work hardest on those sections that will help you most, the checked ones. We suggest that you go through all the sections, but do the unchecked ones quickly, spending more time on lessons that you seem to need.

1.4 Summary

A. It is important for you to spell well. Poor spelling cannot be ignored; it can adversely affect grades and job prospects.

B. Programmed instruction is useful for several reasons. It is efficient; it makes frequent review possible; it allows students to skip instruction that they already know; it requires verbalization, which aids memory.

C. There is no one learning method that works for all students. You may have an eye memory, an ear memory, a muscle memory, or a logical memory. Learn which one works best for you, but use them all.

D. The diagnostic exercises gave you your own spelling profile. This profile told you what kinds of mistakes you make and the lessons on which you should spend the most time and effort in Chapters 3 through 7.

Exercise 1.5

The words in this exercise appeared either in the diagnostic exercises or in the opening discussion. They are words that are very frequently misspelled in student papers. Underline the correct spelling in the parentheses. Then check your work with the answers at the back of the book.

Example: It is (to, <u>too</u>) late to go to the film.

1. There are three (<u>companies</u>, companys) that sell office supplies to the college.

2. I (recieved, <u>received</u>) two B's in the summer session.

3. It takes more (then, <u>than</u>) a logical mind to be a lawyer.

4. The natural (enviroment, <u>environment</u>) of this state is threatened by pollution.

5. The play was not a (tradgedy, <u>tragedy</u>).

6. (<u>Today's</u>, Todays) popular music uses few acoustic instruments.

7. (Alot, <u>A lot</u>) of times the schedules contain errors.

8. It is (<u>really</u>, realy) important to check your math on tax forms.

9. The floodlights are (shining, shinning) on the fountain.

10. There are people (among, amoung) you who have great potential for leadership.

Exercise 1.6

Underline the correct spelling in the parentheses. Check your answers with the answer key at the back of the book.

1. It is (probaly, probably) unnecessary to rewrite your concluding paragraphs.

2. It is easy to (loose, lose) track of time in an exam.

3. It is (fourty, forty) miles to Salem.

4. Is your (roommate, roomate) from the West Coast?

5. (They're, Their) votes must be counted too.

6. The (grammer, grammar) is correct in this article.

7. The metals appear (similar, similiar) to the naked eye.

8. She (definately, definitely) will speak at the meeting.

9. It is hard to (realize, realise) that spring has arrived.

10. She is (makeing, making) a proposal for a grade change.

Chapter **2**
Proofreading

Very early in the research that led to the preparation of this book, we learned that dictated spelling lists were little test of spelling ability. In a series of studies using three spelling tests with exactly the same words in them, we learned that if we dictated the words, the average score was about 90 percent. When we put the words in tests like those in Exercises 1.1, 1.2, and 1.3 in Chapter 1, we learned that the average dropped to 80 percent. When, misspelling the same words, we put them in a paragraph, we learned that the average dropped to about 60 percent. This told us that students may know how to spell certain words but get them wrong in themes or other written exercises. We deduced that an important part of learning how to spell is to learn how to proofread—and that is what we now intend to help you do.

Proofreading is a skill. You will not improve if you merely try to "be careful." It is something that you must learn, something that you must practice, practice, and practice. Its rewards are great.

2.1 Proofreading

To spell accurately, you must have three qualities:

1. You must know how to spell the word.

2. You must write the word correctly on the paper.

3. If you do not, you must catch the error when you proofread.

It is not trait 1 that causes trouble for students; 85 percent of the misspellings in student themes are caused by numbers 2 and 3. Students do write carelessly, and they tend not to be good proofreaders.

Skilled proofreading is college work. It is, moreover, a marketable skill; a good proofreader can earn money. And if the word gets around that you can guarantee immaculate written reports, you will find yourself on powerful committees.

To become a good speller, you have to act like a good speller; your behavior may have to change. To be a good speller, you must always read in two ways. You will always read for content: When you read for content, you are trying to understand and remember.

The second way that you must read is as a proofreader. When you first set your ideas down, you are a writer. Then you must be an editor and proofreader, a person who reads and seeks to improve all parts of the writing, including the central idea, the structure, and the language. You are concerned with word choice, grammar, punctuation, and spelling.

To become a good proofreader for spelling, you have to get into the habit of always noting misspelling. When you see the name of a film, *The Boys Are Alright*, you should smile with a superior feeling. *You* know that it should be two words, *all right*. You know there is the word *altogether,* but you know there are no words spelled *alwrong,* or *alright*. They should be *all wrong* and *all right*.

Note this sentence: "When I moved to the dormatory which accomodates atheletes, my new roomate told me alot about why the university is embarassed more often by jocks then by other students." In this sentence have been inserted some of the misspellings that a teacher of writing sees almost every week. The words should be *dormitory, accommodates, athletes, roommate, a lot, embarrassed,* and *than.* The reason that students misspell these words so often is that their proofreader's eye and ear·are not finely tuned. The words not only should *look* wrong, they should *sound* wrong. As you read with your proofreader mind turned on, your ears must be as attentive as your eyes. Pronounced as they were in the quoted sentence, all the words should grate on your ear.

2.2 Phonics

To be a good proofreader, you need to know something about sounds. Information about the sounds of language is called phonics, and that is what you will be studying from time to time in this book.

What are the vowels?

The vowels are: a, e, i, o, u.

How are vowels different from consonants?

You make vowel sounds without closing or constricting your voice equipment.

To make a consonant, you touch tongue to teeth, as in the case of t, or lips together, as in the case of *m,* or constrict speech flow as in *d* or *h.*

Go through the alphabet aloud, noting how you make all the vowels and consonants.

23

Better Spelling

What is a "long vowel sound"? Give the long sound of each vowel.

The long sound of a vowel exactly represents its name. When you said the vowels aloud, *a, e, i, o,* and *u,* you gave their long sounds.

How is the sound of a consonant different from the sound of a vowel?

To make a consonant sound, you close or constrict part of the speech mechanism through which sound travels; you make a vowel sound by passing air through your speech mechanism with little or no change.

Do you see, then, that a *y* could be a consonant or a vowel? A *y* ending the word *happy* makes the sound of a long *e.*

Can you give some examples of *y* when it makes a consonant sound?

Examples include *you, young, yolk,* and *yellow.*

Remember that we are thinking about sounds, not merely letters. We are talking about "phonics."

Which of these words have the long a sound: *mat, mate, later, latter?*

The long sound of *a* is in *mate* and *later.*

Remembering that we are talking about sounds, and not merely letters, which words have the long sound of a: *bait, bat, eight, play, vein, plea, gray, grey, tap, tape?*

The long *a* sound occurs in *bait, eight, play, vein, gray, grey,* and *tape.*

The lesson here is that you can spell the long a sound in various ways. In the following examples the italicized letters show several ways of spelling the long a sound:

b*ai*t, *eigh*t, pl*ay*, v*ei*n, gr*ay*, gr*ey*, and t*a*pe.

Obviously one of your tasks will be to learn how to spell all English sounds—and how to select the appropriate spellings.

If you are to improve your spelling, you need to go beyond hit or miss or trial and error—learning one word at a time. Instead, to catch up, you need to correct whole classes of words. You will need to be able to think in the abstract about spelling; you will need to understand the concepts used in spelling instruction.

2.3 Diacritical Marks

When you check the dictionary to see how a word is pronounced, you find little markings to show how to sound the letters. In most dictionaries long vowel sounds are indicated by a line across the top; thus the pronunciation of *mate* is shown as māt. The mark above the *a* is called a diacritical mark.

Better Spelling

Can you define "diacritical mark"?

A diacritical mark is one that shows how a letter, or collection
of letters, or a word is sounded.

In the study of phonics, there is a word for sounds that are
or can be used in a language. A *phoneme* is a sound that occurs
in a language. The word *pit* has three sounds, or three
phonemes, one from each letter. The word *phone,* although it
has five letters, has only three phonemes, which are shown in
the dictionary as *fōn.* The phoneme *f* can be spelled *f* or *ph.*
Although the English alphabet has twenty-six letters, the
English language has about forty-five phonemes, some of
which occur in other languages, and some of which do not.
Other languages have their own phonemes, or used sounds,
some of which do not occur in English. In German, for instance, there is the phoneme that we would spell *schn,* which
English does not have. We now use that phoneme for words
that have come into English from German, like *Schneider* and
Wiener schnitzel.

What is a *phoneme?*

A phoneme is a sound that is characteristic to, and used in, a
language.

So far we know what phonics is, what phonemes and long
vowels are, and what a diacritical mark is. From time to time
you will be given more information about phonics as you need it.
Now is the time to get in the habit of learning what
phonemes actually occur in a word and of making sure that
you get all the phonemes into the word.

How do you spell the word that you use to identify the
person who lives in a dormitory with you? You might say,

"The person who shares a dormitory room with me is my
_____."

_____

The word is *roommate.*

If you always spell it right, it is because you hear all the
phonemes, including the *m's* of both *room* and *mate.*

Chances are that you spelled the word right, but many,
many students, when they use the word in writing, leave out
one *m.* The reason is that they have not become sensitive to the
exact pronunciation of the word. They do not know what
phonemes should be included in the word.

● ●

2.4 Syllabification
● ●

To master pronunciation, you must master syllabification,
which is the understanding and proper construction of syllables. A syllable is a letter or group of letters forming one complete uninterrupted unit of speech. Expressed another way, a
syllable is one or more phonemes making up a single, uninterrupted sound, forming either a total word as *man,* or a commonly recognized division of a word, as in *A-mer-i-can.* A syllable can be one word as in *a, an, no,* or *pan.* The one-syllable
word can have only a vowel in it, as in the word *a.* A one-syllable word can be a consonant followed by a vowel, as in *no,* or
a vowel followed by a consonant, as in *on* or *an.* One-syllable
words can have an initial (beginning) consonant and a final
consonant with a vowel in the middle, as in *man.*

When you proofread for spelling, you must sound out every
syllable. Teachers may ask very poor spellers to put a visible
dot above each syllable, like this: The tea/cher may ask him or
her to put a vis/i/ble/ dot a/bove each syl/la/ble.

Read this sentence phonically. To help you check all sounds,
put a mark above every syllable and a mark between syllables:

___

27

Better Spelling

The automobile and the television are part of an important revolution in America today.

This is what your marks should look like:
Thė / aủ/tȯ/mȯ/bilė / aṅd / thė / tėl/ė/vi/siȯn / aŕe / pȧrt / of / aṅ / iṁ/pȯr/tȧnt / rėv/ȯ/lủ/tiȯn / iṅ / Ȧ/mėr/i/cȧ / tȯ/daỷ.

Single syllables can have combinations of phonemes, like *on, eight, of, off, slow, slip, play*. Do you see why the preceding words have one syllable while the following words have two syllables: *upon, eighty, often, play-off, slowly, slipping,* and *playful?*

How many syllables do the following words have: *might, then, than, dine, sign, seen, phone, day, aid, flood, odd, to, too, tot, dot, dote ?*

All the words have just one syllable.

How many syllables do the following words have: *plenty, mighty, dinning, dining, cosign, phony, daily, aiding, flooding, oddly, truly, dotting, doting?*

They all have just two syllables.

Now go back over the words and put a line between the two syllables.

Did you put *plent-y* or *plen-ty? Might-y* or *migh-ty, dail-y* or *dai-ly?*

For our purposes now it does not matter which you decided. All we need now is your awareness that you find two syllables. When you spell the words, you would make sure that all sounds are there. The other syllables are *din-ning, din-ing, co-sign, phon-y, dai-ly, aid-ing, flood-ing, odd-ly, tru-ly, dot-ting, do-ting.*

Now let's see how knowing syllables helps with spelling.

How do you spell the word beginning with *v* describing the sweeper that a housekeeper uses to clean rugs?

Vacuum.

If you spelled it right, you are off to a good start. If you spelled it right, you probably pronounced it correctly.

How many syllables does it have? Spell it correctly, sounding out the syllables as you write:

It has three syllables: *vac-ū-um.*

In between the freshman and junior years of college is the class beginning with *s.* Spell it out: soph_____

Sophomore.

How many syllables does the word have?

It has three: *soph-o-more.*

Better Spelling

As part of your spelling technique, you may wish to get into the habit of a special pronunciation that accentuates the proper spelling. When you are checking the spelling, think to yourself: *soph-O-more.* Accent the middle syllable, made by a single vowel.

Which spelling is correct: *seperate / separate?*

The correct spelling is *separate.* You may wish to help yourself remember this by emphasizing the middle syllable: *sep-A-rate.*

Let's see how you are doing. As you proofread the following paragraph, sound out each word and each syllable to make sure that your eye finds all the sounds that your ear expects. Insert missing sounds.

My roomate, who is a sophmore, realy spent alot of money to buy a vacume cleaner for his mother. I think it is alright for him to do this because she is sick and may not live much longer. In fact, she was not expected to live longer then his father, but she has. I tired to help my roomate raise the money, and I am glad I did.

Did you find the misspellings that we have been trying to eliminate? The words should be *roommate, sophomore, a lot, vacuum, all right,* and *than.* We hope also that you tried out the phonic method on the rest of the words and that you caught misspellings of *really* and *tried. Tired* and *tried,* when sounded out, are different words. Your ear should warn you of this. Adding *-ly* to words is a bit complicated (and will be discussed later in Chapter 5), but it is important now that you thought of how the word sounds, two syllables, *real-ly.*

Exercise 2.1

Now, to try some syllabification, read through this paragraph. As you proofread for spelling, try to find the mistakes by reading sounds and syllables. Put the correct spelling in the right margin. Check your answers with the answer key at the back of the book. Note that some lines may have no errors and some may have more than one error.

1. _____ A problem which has developed in the

2. _____ competative sports world is the transpertation of

3. _____ proffessional atheletes from one major city to

4. _____ another. The mathmetics of the differant

5. _____ problems, the cost of air travel, the price of

6. _____ hotels and meals, and the interpertation of rules

7. _____ and regulations regarding the differance between

8. _____ first class and economy class are definately a

9. _____ problem. It used to be pleasent, probly no

10. _____ problem at all, but now the demand for dignaty

11. _____ by stars just is not appreciated by the modern

12. _____ sports fan, no matter how much he studies the

13. _____ sports pages and magizines. The recignition of

14. _____ sports stars, the Pete Roses, the Jerry Rices, the

15. _____ Michael Jordans, and the Warren Moons brings

16. _____ enough anxiaties, but determaning how to get

17. _____ seven-foot beds and vegetarian meals is an even

18. _____ worse problem. To keep their charges happy is

19. _____ where the manager puts the emphisis. Stars,

20. _____ once accustomed to an acedemic enviornment,

21. _____ must now accept the goverment of the

22 _____ professional discipline, but there is still no

23. _____ substatute for a satisfied superstar.

Exercise 2.2

Do not look back at the paragraph you just proofread; look at the following sets of words and mark which words are spelled correctly. Sound out the syllables. Put circles around the correct versions. Check your answers with the answer key at the back of the book.

1. athelete, athlete

2. transpertation, transportation

3. interpretation, interpertation

4. mathmatics, mathamatics, mathematics

5. pleasant, pleasent

6. recognition, recignition, reconition

7. probibly, probably, probly

8. determining, determaning

9. emphasis, emphesis, emphisis

10. magazines, magizines

11. proffesional, professional

12. anxiaties, anxieties

13. different, differant, diffrent

14. definitely, definately

15. dignity, dignety, dignaty

16. competative, competive, competetive, competitive

17. academic, acidemic

18. enviroment, enviorment, environment

19. goverment, government

20. substatute, substatitue, substitute

••

2.5 The "Spelling Fix": S-P-E-L-L
••

How did you do with your original proofreading? Since these words are frequently misspelled in college papers, it is not surprising if you missed some of them. Remember, though, that words taken from college themes are words that are necessary for college work. They must be mastered. Go back over those that you missed, concentrating on one word at a time. To get the spellings firmly in your mind, you must do the following:

1. Stare at the word; train your eye to expect the right form of the word.

2. Sound out the word, perhaps exaggerating the vowels, the consonants, and the syllables. Train your ear to expect the correct sounds.

3. Write out the word, if not actually in pencil or ink, at least in your mind. Think how the word looks in your own handwriting. Train your hand muscles to write the word, just as you train your muscles to ski or skate.

4. You may wish to help yourself remember by a memory device—called a *mnemonic*—or perhaps by an exaggerated pronunciation (se-PAR-ate), or by some other association. One student remembers *sOph-O-mOre,* by thinking of the three *o*'s as the open eyes and mouth of a startled sOphOmOre.

In this way you train your eye's memory, your ear's memory, your muscle's memory, and your intelligence's memory. Try the word you have just encountered: *mnemonic.*

1. *Stare* at it, and note at once that there is a strange first letter.

2. *Pronounce* it, exaggerating the first letter: *mmmmmm-ne-mon-ic.*

3. *Engrave* the word. Write it down firmly and slowly. Close your eyes and write the word out in your mind; write it out on paper again slowly and firmly.

4. *Look* for a *link,* an association, perhaps saying to yourself, "An mmmmmm-ne-mon-ic helps remember. I must re-mmmmmemmmmm-ber the *m* even though it is silent."

As time passes, you may discover which one of your memories is the strongest, and you may come to rely upon it. Until you can depend on just one of your senses, though, you must get in the habit of working all of them.

What are the first letters of the key words in the preceding list: *stare, pronounce, engrave, look,* and *link?* The answer is S-P-E-L-L. Now you have a mnemonic device to help you remember the steps in the "spelling fix."

• •
2.6 Use of the Dictionary
• •

This book is organized to help you solve your most important problems first. Since writers actually know how to spell most of the words they misspell, you worked on the technique of proofreading. There does, however, come the time when you have to look up the word for the first time, when you wish to check a word about which you are uncertain, or when you wish to use the dictionary to confirm the spelling of some rarely used word like *sesquipedalian, efficacy,* or *eradicate.*

The dictionary is the most important reference work on the desk of any writer; few professional writers are ever without one. You must become skilled not only in finding words and getting the correct spelling but also in figuring out a method to remember the dictionary's spelling.

Most college students can find a word in a dictionary. If, on occasion, you cannot find a word, you may be encountering the troubles with phonemes mentioned earlier. It would be good if *fotograf* were spelled that way, but it is not; it is *photograph.* It would be convenient if *pneumonia* began with *n,* but it does not. If you cannot find a word, then you must experiment with spellings that the sounds suggest. As you go through the lessons in this text, you will find suggestions about how to do this.

Above all, you must try to prevent the problem of having to locate a word in the dictionary. When you first encounter a word with a tricky spelling, take the time to fix the spelling in

Better Spelling

your mind. Remember *mnemonic?* The best way to do this is to use the "spelling fix": *s*tare, *p*ronounce, *e*ngrave, *l*ook, and *l*ink (spell) with your muscle memory, your eye memory, your ear memory, and your intelligence memory. In spelling bees, students of long ago chanted out the spelling of *Mississippi: m-I-ss-I-ss-I-pp-I,* with the vowels accented and the double consonants hurried. Read as a speller: *se-PAR-ate, gram-MAR, calen-DAR, di-AR-rhea, ex-is-TENCE.* If you hear a new word in class, ask your instructor how to spell it; then fix it in your mind.

When you do look up a word in the dictionary, use the "fix" technique. For years students have been told to write out a new word three or five times — but we have yet to know a single student who does that consistently. (You may expect no more of yourself, but you can expect yourself to write it out *once,* and imagine yourself writing it several times more, pronouncing the syllables carefully.) Stare at the word and say it to yourself. You are saving yourself time if you do not have to look it up again. Think of *vac-u-UM, ne-ces-sary, ap-PEN-dix, person-nel, pseud-o-nym, venge-ance, serge-ant* or *super-SEDE.*

In particular, you should be careful about the words that have a single-vowel syllable in the middle of the word. Very often the dictionary key shows these words with the vowel sound indicated by a *schwa* (ə). An example is *complimentary,* which is shown as ͵*käm-plə-ˋment-ə-rē.* When you memorize the spelling of the word, note the primary accent (´) on *ment;* the secondary accent (͵) on *kom,* which receives the second hardest accent; and the syllabification (*com-pli-men-ta-ry*). You should note the schwa sound. Write the word out, stare at it, spell it to yourself, and accent a sound that indicates how the middle vowel phonemes are represented: com-plI-mEn-tary. Be sure to get the meaning clear: Stress the difference between *com-plI-men-tary,* which means "flattering," and *com-plE-men-tary,* which means "completing" or "supplying needs or deficiencies." Other examples include *em-bar-rass,* which is shown as *im-ˈbar-ə s,* and *laminate,* which is shown as *ˈlam-ə-nāt* but which you may wish to think of as *lam-IN-ate,* as you think of *de-FIN-Ite,* which is shown as ‘*def-* ə *-nat* using the pronunciation key.

So there it is, your first extended lesson in spelling. We have said that every time you encounter a difficult word, you should go through the multisense system of fixing the spelling in your mind. Do not wait to miss the word before you catalog it in the difficult-to-spell class. If a word seems difficult to spell, go to work on it. Write it out. Stare at it. Think of writing it out again. Pronounce it several times, or *over*pronounce it.

Let's see how you have been doing. In the past pages you have encountered some troublemaker words. Next you'll find some of the misspellings that have just been discussed as well as others that are new but will give you practice in fixing words other students have had difficulty spelling.

Exercise 2.3

Proofread the following paragraph, putting the correct spelling for misspelled words in the blanks provided. Note that not all lines will have errors, and some may have more than one. Check your answers with the answer key.

1. _____ When the shades of night actualy

2. _____ look differant in Newark, when the

3. _____ dull turns to white of arteficial illumination,

4. _____ when the goverment buildings empty

5. _____ and everyone becomes an athelete running

6. _____ in compatition for the trolley cars,

7. _____ when no one is embarassed to ask someone to

8. _____ punch the time clock, when if a photagraph

9. _____ were taken it would show no one even
reletively

10. _____ pleasent, when everyone would rather read a magizine

11. _____ than pass a complement to his or her neighbor,

12. _____ when all these things are happening,

13. _____ and besides — when alot of heavy men get

14. _____ into street cars frist and all the lean

15. _____ men have their dayly climb over them, when

16. _____ the salespeople in the store think it alright

17. _____ to lock there cash register just as

18. _____ you rush up to the counter, when the man

19. _____ who has just bought a suberban house stops

20. _____ at a wholesale meat market jist to

21. _____ have a laugh because he bought a cheap stake,

22. _____ when the pollice officer turns away from the

23. _____ trolley that has to many people in it,

24. _____ then it is that the city changes. Then

25. _____ it is that night life beggins.

What you must do now is to use your instruction about proofreading, your knowledge of vowels, consonants, syllables, phonics, and mnemonics as you work your way through the rest of this book. Remember to use all your senses, as you get into the habit of practicing the spelling fix: *s*tare, *p*ronounce, *e*ngrave, *l*ook, and *l*ink.

2.7 Summary

A. To spell accurately, you must have three qualities:
   1. You must know how to spell the word.
   2. You must write the word correctly.
   3. If you do not write a word correctly, you must catch the error when you proofread.

B. Eighty-five percent of the errors that occur in student themes are a result of careless writing and/or inadequate proofreading.

C. A good proofreader for spelling gets into the habit of noting misspellings. The eyes sense when a word looks wrong, and the ears sense when a word sounds wrong.

D. To learn to proofread, you need to know something about phonics—the sounds of the language—and how these sounds are reproduced in writing.

E. As you proofread for spelling, use the technique of syllabification. Read the sounds and syllables of each word.

F. To get the correct spelling of a word firmly in your mind, use the "spelling fix."
   1. Train your eye to expect the right form of the word.
   2. Train your ear to expect the correct sound of the word.
   3. Train your hand muscles to expect the correct feeling when you write the word.
   4. Use mnemonics (memory devices) to remember a tricky spelling. You can use the handy acronym, S-P-E-L-L, to remind yourself of the process of the spelling fix.

      S Stare at the word.
      P Pronounce the word, exaggerating the syllables.
      E Engrave the word, writing it carefully and firmly.
      L Look for a
      L Link, an association, or mnemonic device that will help you remember the spelling.

G. The dictionary is your most important reference source.

Better Spelling

Exercise 2.4

Underline the correct spelling in the parentheses. When you have finished, check your work with the answers at the back of the book.

Example: Use a (<u>mnemonic</u>, nemonic) device on the word.

1. There is no such thing as a perfect (vacume, vacuum).

2. Next semester she will have (sophmore, sophomore) status.

3. (Separate, Seperate) the answer sheet into two parts.

4. It is (alright, all right) to take your exam during the first session.

5. The board of directors (tired, tried) to merge the two companies.

6. Some (athletes, atheletes) qualify for professional contracts through "hardship" status.

7. The city's public (transportation, transpertation) system is being renovated.

8. The diplomats are housed in a (goverment, government) facility.

9. (Vengance, Vengeance) is mandatory according to his cultural values.

10. The (suberban, suburban) towns line the river to the east and west of the city.

Chapter 3

Three Major Rules

3.1 Ei or ie?

Exercise 3.1

Proofread the paragraph for spelling errors, writing the correct spelling in the blanks provided. Note that some lines may have no errors and others may have more than one. Check your answers with the answer key before proceeding.

1. _____ At the hieght of the morning rush hour

2. _____ the financiers stand at the station

3. _____ platform, a breifcase in one hand, an

4. _____ umbrella in the other. The city waits

5. _____ to recieve them. Their goals are to

6. _____ acheive success and to receive

7. _____ promotions and higher salaries. They

Better Spelling

8. _____ cannot conceive of yeilding to any

9. _____ obstacle in the path of affluence, but

10. _____ each one longs for a time of leisure, of

11. _____ releif from the world of accounts, bills,

12. _____ and reciepts. No one talks to his

13. _____ nieghbor on the platform, for it is only

14. _____ 8:00 a.m.; each one is silently wieghing

15. _____ his chances for a profitable day. Even

16. _____ when the economy is beseiged by

17. _____ recession and salary ceilings fall, each

18. _____ one believes that he will one day be the

19. _____ cheif of his industry.

How did you do? If you correctly identified all eleven of the errors, skim the remainder of this section and go on to the next section, "Final Consonants: Single or Double?"

If you were unable to spot all of the errors in the paragraph, go very carefully through this section. Be sure that you follow directions precisely. You can use the programmed technique effectively only if you block off the answer spaces as directed. Otherwise you may be tempted to use the answers, thereby greatly reducing your prospects for really learning how to use the rule.

You can greatly increase your chances of spelling *ie* or *ei* words correctly by memorizing this simple rhyme:

Put *i* before *e*
Except after *c*
Or when sounded like *a*
As in *neighbor* and *weigh*.

The first half of this rule applies to words where the vowel combination of *ie* or *ei* is pronounced as a long *ē*. With only a few exceptions, such words are spelled by placing the *i* before the *e*, unless immediately preceded by a *c*.

Examples are *chief, mischief, handkerchief,* and *believe.* Exceptions are *either, neither, leisure, seize, weird, species, protein, caffeine, financier, sheik,* and *Fahrenheit.*

When preceded by a *c*, however, such words are almost *always* spelled by putting the *e* before the *i.* Examples are *receive, conceit,* and *ceiling.* Combine the memories of your eyes, ears, and muscles to form a spelling fix in your mind for these words. When the *c* is pronounced *sh,* as in *ancient* or *efficient,* however, the *i* comes before the *e.* Now proceed to the following exercise.

Exercise 3.2

Insert the correct letters to complete each word. Check your answers before proceeding.

1. The machine is unconcerned about how the p_____ce of metal will come out.

2. The owners and trustees bel_____ve in the long-term security of the organization.

3. When the rec_____ver is placed on the hook, the conversation ends.

4. The electronics f_____ld is the one most likely to create a monster in the disguise of a breakthrough.

5. Most people cannot conc_____ve of an end to space.

6. L_____sure is of value only as a complement to labor.

7. The c_____ling needs painting.

8. There is misch_____f in the dorms on Halloween.

9. She is not at all conc_____ted despite her high marks.

10. N_____ther John nor Jose has returned.

Better Spelling

Did you remember that *leisure* and *neither* are exceptions? The last two lines of the rule tell us that words in which the vowel combination is pronounced as a long *ā* are spelled by putting the *e* before the *i*. Examples given in the rhyme are *neighbor* and *weigh*. Other examples are *neigh, sleigh, eight, weight, inveigle, feint, deign, veil,* and *freight.* Now see how well you have mastered the rule.

Exercise 3.3

Add *ie* or *ei* to complete the words below. Check your answers before proceeding.

1. A low cloud c_____ling holds in the moist, humid air.

2. Dalton set up the first table of atomic w_____ghts.

3. A rec_____pt for all expenses must be included for reimbursement.

4. It was his cunning that helped him to move from petty th_____f to warlord.

5. Thus, the n_____ghboring villages along the border speak each other's language.

6. The test tube w_____ghed less after the experiment.

7. They tried to dec_____ve the customs officer.

8. The fr_____ght car was derailed in Houston.

9. Some Moslem women still wear the v_____l.

10. His n_____ce attended the same college.

Notice that words such as *foreign* and *height* are pronounced with sounds other than the long *ē* or the long *ā*. Such words are usually spelled by putting the *e* before the *i*. Other examples are *forfeit, sleight,* and *surfeit.* Exceptions are *friend, pimiento, die,* and *sieve.*

Now try an exercise that uses those words not covered by the rule-in-rhyme.

Exercise 3.4

Add *ie* or *ei* to complete the words. Check your answers before proceeding.

1. What we call tidal waves are really s_____smic waves.

2. My oil tank was leaking like a s_____ve.

3. Sports reached the h_____ght of power in media programming during the 1970s.

4. *Magic* is only a sensational term for what is really the art of sl_____ght of hand.

5. While it was cheaper to travel to for_____gn countries than it had been a decade earlier, it was much more expensive for food and lodging.

6. The general d_____d before the battle's end.

7. The company had to forf_____t its profits.

8. This olive does not have a pim_____nto.

9. There was a surf_____t of funds in the benefits pool.

10. Her fr_____nd finished writing the last chapter.

Did you remember how *sieve, died, pimiento,* and *friend* are spelled? Now try a review of the whole lesson.

Exercise 3.5

Add *ie* or *ei* to complete the words. Check your answers before proceeding.

Better Spelling

1. The congresswoman f_____lded questions for an hour.
2. The terrified horse n_____ghed all night.
3. At last he perc_____ved the poet's meaning.
4. The pr_____st's training lasted two years.
5. Effic_____ncy is essential in production.
6. _____ther take an exam or write a paper.
7. Her dec_____tfulness finally angered the clerk.
8. The anc_____nt poem was written in runes.
9. Her gr_____f ended abruptly when he was found alive.
10. The force f_____ld will shield the electrodes.

You have, at this point, undergone three very important processes to avoid misspelling words with the *ie* or *ei* vowel combination. First, you have learned the rule. Second, you have seen examples of how each of the various parts of the rule works for large groups of words. And, third, you have used the parts of the rule yourself in three different programs to test your understanding of it.

3.2 Final Consonants: Single or Double?

Exercise 3.6

Proofread the paragraph for spelling errors, writing the correct spelling in the blank provided. Note that not all lines will contain errors. Check your answers before proceeding.

1. _____ For me the first year of college has
2. _____ totaly changed my life. I have had to

3.2 Final Consonants: Single or Double?

3. _____ learn to live in a more self-controlled

4. _____ fashion than I did at home when my

5. _____ parents compeled me to behave

6. _____ reasonably. A few weeks after enterring

7. _____ college I noticed that changes were

8. _____ beginning to take place in me. My

9. _____ appetite drasticly decreased. My

10. _____ appearance mattered very little to me,

11. _____ even though my roomate told me I was

12. _____ getting thinner by the minute. By

13. _____ Thanksgiving I had convinced myself

14. _____ that transfering to a college closer to

15. _____ home was the answer. I got the

16. _____ application forms but never submited

17. _____ them. Now that I look back at this I

18. _____ realize that I was rebeling against the

19. _____ independence I so badly wanted in high

20. _____ school. Somehow, that unforgettable

21. _____ first semester ended. During Christmas

22. _____ vacation a strange thing occured.

23. _____ I actualy missed my lovely room in the

24. _____ dormitory back at school. The home

25. _____ town I had missed so much now

26. _____ seemed clannish and repellent. I was

27. _____ finaly beginning to understand the

28. _____ saying "you can't go home again."

Better Spelling

How did you do? If you missed more than one, you need to work on the programmed lessons on final consonants. If you got them all right or had only one error, briefly survey the lessons below and then go directly to the next section containing information on forming plurals of nouns.

Now you are going to learn and practice one of the most useful spelling rules in our language. It is especially useful because it tells how to spell many words when you add suffixes to them. This rule covers *thousands* of words!

The rule comes in five simple parts:

1. If a word with the *accent on the last (or only) syllable*

2. has a *single final consonant that is*

3. *preceded by a single vowel,*

4. then when *adding a suffix beginning with a vowel*

5. you *double the final consonant.*

Sounds complicated? It's not, especially when you see how it works. Practice with an easy word, *begin*.

1. Is the accent in *begin* on the last syllable?
   yes, *GIN*

2. Does *begin* have a single final consonant?
   yes, *n*

3. Is the final consonant preceded by a short vowel?
   yes, *i*

4. Does the suffix *-ing* begin with a vowel?
   yes, *i*

5. Then, if you add *-ing* to *begin,* do you double the *n*?
   yes, *beginning*

See how it works? Try another word that we all know, *bewilder.*

If you wanted to add a vowel suffix, *-ing,* to *bewilder,* would you double that final *r?*

no

Why not? It has a single final consonant that is preceded by a vowel.

Because the accent is on the middle syllable, not on the last: *be WILDer*

Try another easy word, *hot.*

1. We know immediately that it is a word that has only one syllable.

2. Does it end in a final consonant?

   yes, *t*

3. Is the final consonant preceded by a single short vowel?

   yes, *o*

4. Do the suffixes *-er* and *-est* begin with vowels?

   yes, both

5. If you add *-er* or *-est* to hot, do you double the *t?*

   yes, *hotter, hottest*

Now look at a word, *prefer,* which presents a slightly tricky problem.

Suppose you want to add *-ing* to *prefer.* The *accent is on the last syllable* and there is a *single final consonant preceded by a single vowel.*

If you add the vowel suffix *-ing,* do you double the *r?*

yes, *preferring*

49

Better Spelling

Now suppose you want to add the suffix *-ence* to *prefer.* *Say* the word *with* the suffix aloud. Has the accent moved?

yes

Where is the accent now?

on the first syllable, *PRE*

Do you double the consonant *r* when adding *-ence,* then?

no, *PREference*

This shows you why the location of the accented syllable in a word is important in spelling. In a few words, like *prefer,* the accent can *shift* from one syllable to another when you add a suffix.

Now that you are familiar with the rule, look at an exception to the rule, the word *transfer.* Even though the accent is commonly placed on the *first* syllable and not the *last,* you double the *r* when adding vowel suffixes.

1. Spell *transfer + -ed*

transferred

2. Spell *transfer + -ing*

transferring

You may wish to help remember the proper spelling by accenting the final syllable, *transFER,* which actually is the preferred pronunciation.

A different kind of exception is found in the word *excel.*

If you want to add to it the vowel suffix *-ing,* do you use one *l* or two *ll*'s, according to this rule?

two *l*'s, *excelling*

And if you want to add the vowel suffix *-ence,* you see that the accent shifts to which syllable in the word?

first, *excellence*

Still, you double the *l.* Remember that there are very few exceptions such as the ones above, and they can easily be memorized by using the spelling fix: concentration on eye, ear, and muscle memories. Now *test the rule* by doing the following exercises.

Exercise 3.7

In the following sentences spell the words with the suffixes added. Check your answers before proceeding.

1. TV is an (excel + ent) _____ example of media power.

2. The (transmit + ing) _____ equipment is extraordinarily complex.

3. Our TV habits are compulsive and random, not (plan + ed) _____ .

4. Children are not (equip + ed) _____ to make sound judgments about what they watch.

5. What is (repel + ent) _____ to one viewer may be entertaining to another.

6. (Win + ing) _____ the election was most important.

7. His books were (forgot + en) _____ .

8. A (lessen + ing) _____ of the tensions was achieved.

9. The whistle will blow at (quit + ing) _____ time.

10. Her (reason + ing) _____ powers are excellent.

11. In summer (unsweet + ened) _____ juice is best.

12. The union leaders had a (heat + ed) _____ argument.

13. Smoking is not (permit + ed) _____ here.

14. Both students were (expel + ed) _____ for plagiarism.

15. The troops were (forbid + en) _____ to enter.

16. The (rebel + ion) _____ was suppressed.

17. Cheating must be (curtail + ed) _____ at all costs.

18. Our (digit + al) _____ computer is broken.

19. The wrestler (pin + ed) _____ both opponents.

20. The professor (allot + ed) _____ enough time to finish.

More on Final Consonants

1. When the letters *f* and *l* are at the end of monosyllables and come immediately after single vowels, they are usually doubled. Examples are *staff, cliff, puff, all, bell, hill,* and *null.* There are a few exceptions, including *clef, if, of,* and *pal.* If any of these words is unfamiliar, give it the spelling fix.

2. The letter *s,* at the end of a monosyllable and coming after a single vowel is also usually doubled. Examples are *grass, press, hiss, mass, moss, truss,* and *toss.* Exceptions include *as, gas, yes, his, this, pus, plus, bus, thus,* and *us.*

3. The consonants *b, d, g, m, n, p, r, t,* and *z* are the only others that are doubled at the end of a word. Examples include *ebb, add, odd, egg, Ann, inn, Finn, err, burr, purr, putt,* and *fizz.* Note that *net* and *set* are exceptions.

3.2 Final Consonants: Single or Double?

4. A consonant is rarely doubled if it occurs at the end of a word and just after a diphthong or a double vowel. A diphthong is a double vowel sound. In the word *toy*, the final sound, if repeated slowly, sounds like *oh-ee*. In the word *cow*, the final sound is a diphthong; it sounds like *ah-oo*. Even the long *i* sound is a diphthong. When you say "I am a human being," the first word sounds like *"Ah-ee."* In the word *pail*, the two vowels go together to make a diphthong, sounding like *aye-ee*. The words *all, peat, mail, haul, door, maim, poor, sweat*, and *clean* are examples of single consonants following either double vowels or diphthongs. Exceptions are rare, and they tend to be recently borrowed foreign words or scientific words. The word guess is really not an exception because the *u* is part of the phoneme *gu*, which makes the *g* a hard sound (different from the word *gestation*, which begins with a sound like the *j* in *just*).

5. Monosyllables ending with the sound of *k* are not consistent. Usually a vowel just before the sound is followed by a *ck*, as in *black, fleck, click, knock*, and *buck*, but the words *sac, talc, tic, zinc, arc*, and *disc* are exceptions. Now, to check your mastery of this principle, proofread the paragraph in this exercise.

Exercise 3.8

Write the correct spelling in the blank provided for any line containing an error. Check your answers before proceeding.

1. _____ The shepherd's energy began

2. _____ to eb as he hauled himself

3. _____ up to the ledge. The swet

4. _____ pored from his brow. Below him the

Better Spelling

5. _____ cliff stretched down a thousand meters.

6. _____ Raising himself up, he swung his star

7. _____ in a wide ark over his head in triumph.

Exercise 3.9

Underline the correct spelling in the pairs below. Check your answers before proceeding.

1. zink, zinc
2. disc, disk
3. gas, gass
4. geuss, guess
5. flec, fleck

6. nul, null
7. clef, cleft
8. od, odd
9. fizz, fiz
10. purr, pur

Derivatives

Derivatives are words formed from a base word. Some changes in derivatives are inflections, that is, changes in words to form plurals, such as *box, boxes; man, men;* and *medium, media.* Other inflections are changes to form tenses of verbs, such as *ride, rode, ridden; do, did, done;* and *is, was, been.* Still others change to form possessives like *he, his; they, theirs;* and *girl, girl's,* and *girls'.* Other inflections change adjectives to adverbs *(dark, darkly),* nouns to adjectives *(woman, womanish),* nouns to adverbs *(woman, womanly),* and verbs to verbals *(jump, jumping, jumped).*

1. Words ending in a vowel followed by *c* often require a *k* before a suffix, like *panic, panicking; picnic, picnicking;*

colic, colicky; traffic, trafficking; and *frolic, frolicked.* To make the plurals of these words, simply add an *s: panics, picnics, colics, traffics.* Fix carefully on these spellings.

Exercise 3.10

Underline the correct spelling in the pairs below. Check your answers before proceeding.

1. panicing, panicking
2. trafficking, traffiking
3. froliced, frolicked
4. coliky, colicky
5. picnicking, picnicing

6. picnic, picnick
7. riden, ridden
8. frolick, frolic
9. medias, media
10. froliking, frolicking

2. Some base words and derivatives that you should be able to spell as a result of your work in the first part of this chapter are *clan, clannish; plan, planned, planning, planner; bag, baggage; hot, hotter, hottest; wit, witty; abet, abetted, abetting, abettor; begin, beginning, beginner; infer, inferred, inferring.*

   The effect of doubling the consonant is the retention of the short vowel sound. Note the difference in sounds between *canned, caned; taped, tapped; hoping, hopping.*

Exercise 3.11

To demonstrate your understanding of this principle, underline the word in the second or third column that rhymes with the word in the first column. For some words you may find no rhyme, in which case you will write "none" beside it. Check your answers before proceeding.

Better Spelling

1. sitter	fighter	fitter
2. roper	topper	toper
3. fated	sated	matted
4. dropping	topping	roping
5. forgetting	deleting	regretting
6. cured	heard	purred
7. madden	maiden	McFadden
8. petting	repeating	letting
9. bitten	heighten	mitten
10. witty	city	flighty

This exercise was not supposed to be difficult; its purpose was to let you focus on how the word sounds when you add a suffix after a single consonant following a vowel: If you wish to retain the short vowel sound, you double the consonant. Did you think that *city-witty* is an exception to the rule? Not so. The rule applies only when you have a *base word* to which you are adding a suffix. This rule is about derivatives.

How would you spell the adjective made from *man* and ending with *-ish?*

The spelling is *mannish.*

This word actually exists. In contrast to *male, masculine, manly,* and *manful, mannish* is unfavorable or pejorative. *Mannish* means that the male traits are affected by a woman in an unpleasant way. The derivative is made with a doubled consonant. It rhymes with *vanish,* which is not a derivative, and thus does not come under the derivative rule.

How then, do you spell the opposite word, describing a man who acts like a woman?

The answer is *womanish*. It means effeminate.

Do you see why *mannish* and *womanish* do not violate the rule? Think the answer out and write it here.

The answer is that *man* is a single-syllable word, and the rule applies when you add a suffix. *Woman* ends with a vowel sound and a consonant, but—and this you must watch—the accent is not on the final syllable.

The same syllable, if accented, would have required a doubled consonant. In the novel *Beau Geste,* when the soldiers returned to their duty, the author said that they "re-manned their posts," and the word he apparently coined rhymed with *demand* instead of *remained.*

We hope that all this talk about sounds and rhymes is not tiring you. It is very important that you become sensitive about sounds, syllables, and letters; that is why we are paying so much attention to them.

A final word: Remember that this rule applies only to final consonants preceded by a single vowel sound. It does not apply to words that have double vowels or diphthongs. Can you think of some examples?

Examples: *need, needy; briefer, briefest.*

Why does the rule not apply to *act, actor?*

Because the base word has two final consonants.

57

Better Spelling

Why does the rule not apply to *profit / profiting?*

Because the accent is on the first syllable.

Which is the right derivative of *travail,* which means "trouble" or "distress"? *Travailed, or travailled?* Why?

The word is *travailed.* The accent is on the final syllable, but the sound before the consonant is a diphthong, a double vowel sound, which comes out like *"aye-ee."*

You may see some words like *kidnaped, equaled, labeled, paralleled,* and *worshiped* that are confusing because you might think that the consonant should be doubled. Use the spelling fix to hold the proper spellings in your mind. You may see words where the final syllable is not accented, and the consonant is doubled; for instance, *biassed, cancelled, carolled, channelled, chiselled, pencilled, perilled, quarrelled, ravelled, revelled, rivalled, shrivelled, travelling,* and *tunnelling.* These apparent exceptions will appear in publications printed in England; most American dictionaries list them as acceptable alternates.

Exercise 3.12

Underline the correct spelling in the pairs below. Check your answers before proceeding.

1. picnick, picnic
2. panicking, paniking
3. dropping, droping
4. regretted, regreted
5. forgeting, forgetting

6. madening, maddening
7. remited, remitted
8. forgotten, forgoten
9. babysiter, babysitter
10. baggage, bagage

●●

3.3 Forming Plurals of Nouns

●●●

Exercise 3.13

As you proofread the paragraph for spelling errors, write the correct spelling in the blank provided for any line containing an error. Check your answers before proceeding.

1. _____ The reason why people follow normes

2. _____ is so that human societys will have

3. _____ some kind of order in them. Most

4. _____ people agree that norms are necessary,

5. _____ but some feel that it is unfair that

6. _____ there are different norms for a man

7. _____ than for a women. In fact, most

8. _____ feminists believe that a revision of

9. _____ norm structure is one of the keyes to

10. _____ equality between the sexs. Yet sex

11. _____ forms are only one specie of

12. _____ discrimination against women. Women

13. _____ increasingly feel that they must protect

14. _____ themselfs from all social patterns and

15. _____ habits that degrade them, no matter

16. _____ what. While some sociologistes and

17. _____ psychologists are concerned about the

18. _____ future of the family unit, radical

59

Better Spelling

19. _____ feminists claim that most culturs in
20. _____ the world have been divided in halfs for
21. _____ so long that the very idea of unity is a
22. _____ joke.

How did you do? If you identified all of the errors and could spell them correctly, skim the remainder of this section and go on to the next chapter, "Words Commonly Confused." However, if you missed any of the plural spellings, you will need to proceed to the program lessons that follow.

Most of the time, plural nouns are spelled in English simply by adding an *s;* for example, the word *subject* is made plural by adding an *s: subjects.* The same is true for the word *course.* The plural simply adds an *s: courses.* There are several other ways of forming plurals, however, and you need to know them in order to improve your spelling.

1. Some words, like *sex* in the paragraph at the beginning of this section, take an *-es* to form the plural: *sexes.* Words that end in the singular with *ss, sh, ch,* or *x* all require *-es* in becoming plural.

Exercise 3.14

Spell the plural forms for the following words. Check your answers before proceeding.

1. mess_____   6. princess _____
2. latch_____   7. hex _____
3. gash _____   8. mass _____
4. box _____   9. switch_____
5. birch _____   10. wish _____

2. Words such as *bully* that end in a *y* following a consonant are made plural by changing the *y* to *i* and adding -*es: bullies*. If the noun is a proper noun, just add an *s:* "There are two Sallys in my class."

Exercise 3.15

Write the plurals of the following words. Check your answers before proceeding.

1. luxury _____
2. economy _____
3. democracy _____
4. energy _____
5. Mary _____

6. summary_____
7. hypocrisy_____
8. industry_____
9. revolutionary _____
10. Harry _____

3. Words ending in a *y* following a vowel simply add an *s* to form the plural. Thus, *key* becomes *keys* in the plural.

Exercise 3.16

Spell the plurals of the following words. Check your answers before proceeding.

1. turkey _____
2. highway _____
3. holiday _____
4. alloy_____
5. trolley _____

6. boy _____
7. play_____
8. attorney_____
9. chimney_____
10. ray _____

4. Words that end in *f* or *fe* usually add an *s* in making the plural; for example, *belief* becomes *beliefs* in the plural.

Exercise 3.17

Make the following words plural. Check your answers before proceeding.

1. fief _____   6. tiff _____

2. handkerchief _____   7. bluff _____

3. roof _____   8. skiff _____

4. reef _____   9. whiff _____

5. belief _____   10. cliff _____

Some such words, however, are made plural by changing the *f* to *v* and adding *s* or *-es*. Thus, *wife* becomes *wives,* and *elf* becomes *elves.*

Exercise 3.18

Make the following words plural. Check your answers before proceeding.

1. life _____   6. knife _____

2. half _____   7. self _____

3. wolf _____   8. loaf _____

4. shelf _____   9. leaf _____

5. wife _____   10. sheaf _____

There is no obvious rule here, but a dictionary will always tell you how to form the correct plural of nouns that end in *f* or *fe*. Fix the proper form: S-P-E-L-L.

5. For a few words the singular and plural forms are the same. In that category are a number of animal names: *antelope, deer, fish, moose, sheep,* and *trout;* all use the same spelling in the plural as in the singular. *Antelope* may, however, be spelled with an *s, antelopes,* and *fish* with an *-es, fishes,* in the plural. Other words that are the same in both singular and plural form are *Vietnamese, Chinese, and species.*

6. Some old nouns that come from our language's Germanic roots are made plural in unusual ways. Observe how the plurals are formed in the following words:

Singular	Plural	Singular	Plural
child	children	mouse	mice
foot	feet	ox	oxen
goose	geese	tooth	teeth
louse	lice	woman	women
man	men		

7. Most nouns that end in *o* are made plural simply by adding an *s.* Thus, *halo, lasso, salvo, memo, piano,* and *radio* become *halos, lassos, salvos, memos, pianos, and radios.*

Exercise 3.19

Write out the plural forms of the following nouns. Check your answers before proceeding.

1. curio_____   4. banjo_____

2. rodeo _____   5. zero _____

3. studio_____   6. solo _____

Better Spelling

7. soprano _____   9. ratio _____

8. concerto_____   10. stereo _____

A few such nouns, however, take an *-es* in the plural; for example, *cargo, echo, hero, tomato,* and *potato* become *cargoes, echoes, heroes, tomatoes,* and *potatoes.* A dictionary will tell you which plural form to use if you do not already know. The plural form will be shown after the abbreviation *pl.*

Exercise 3.20

Write out the plural forms of these nouns that end in 0. Check your answers.

1. embargo _____   4. tornado_____

2. mosquito_____   5. veto _____

3. Negro_____

Exercise 3.21

Underline the correct plural spelling in each of the pairs that follow. Check your answers.

1. studioes, studios   6. vetoes, vetos

2. zeros, zeroes   7. ratioes, ratios

3. stereoes, stereos   8. banjos, banjoes

4. solos, soloes   9. concertos, concertoes

5. mosquitoes, mosquitos   10. embargoes, embargos

8. Compound plurals are usually formed by making the same change in the key word as when it stands alone; *court-martial, courts-martial; son-in-law, sons-in-law;*

64

knight-errant, knights-errant. When the compound is very common and the elements have the quality of a single word, the plural is made in the usual way: *cupful, cupfuls; handful, handfuls.*

9. One of the most common mistakes in newspapers today involves misuse of the word *media* (television, magazines, newspapers, and other aspects of the information industry referred to collectively as "the media"). *Media* is a plural form of *medium;* therefore, we must say "the media are," never "the media is." Another plural that many use incorrectly as a singular is *criteria;* the singular form is *criterion.*

In your college classes you probably have a *syllabus.* Many people, knowing a little Latin and thinking that the word is from that source, call the plural *syllabi.* This has happened so many times that dictionaries have come to accept the spelling, but—if you really want to be right—you should know that the word comes from the Greek and that the plural should be *syllabuses.*

Some words that are less frequently used but which you might some day write in the plural (and surprise readers by getting them right) are the following:

cherub	cherubim	phenomenon	phenomena
seraph	seraphim	stratum	strata
soliloquy	soliloquies	analysis	analyses
alumnus	alumni	basis	bases
alumna	alumnae	oasis	oases
focus	loci	hypothesis	hypotheses
fungus	fungi	parenthesis	parentheses
radius	radii	thesis	theses
datum	data		

Better Spelling

Exercise 3.22

Write the plural forms of the words. Check your answers before proceeding.

Singular	Plural	Singular	Plural
1. cherub	_____	10. phenomenon	_____
2. seraph	_____	11. stratum	_____
3. soliloquy	_____	12. analysis	_____
4. alumnus	_____	13. basis	_____
5. alumna	_____	14. oasis	_____
6. focus	_____	15. hypothesis	_____
7. fungus	_____	16. parenthesis	_____
8. radius	_____	17. thesis	_____
9. datum	_____		

Exercise 3.23

Make the nouns in parentheses into plurals. Check your answers before proceeding.

1. There are several (monarchy) _____ in Europe today.

2. Members of the press refused to be the (lackey) _____ of the new military government.

3. The (leaf) _____ of deciduous trees are the equivalent of the needles of the conifers.

4. The (roof) _____ were all painted green and yellow for camouflage.

5. Two (moose) _____ a bull and a calf, swam the bay in under two hours.

6. There are more (woman) _____ than men in the world.

7. The (radio) _____ were all turned on at exactly the same time.

8. There are several active (volcano) _____ in the Hawaiian Islands.

9. She had to write two (thesis) _____, one for each degree.

10. The (larva) _____ all had to be destroyed before the rains came to the forest.

11. The (alumna) _____ all wore formal gowns.

12. All the (stereo) _____ are now on sale.

13. Three of the president's (veto) _____ were strongly criticized.

14. Her (daughter-in-law) _____ have all settled in Iowa.

15. (Ox) _____ are still used to pull plows.

16. The cafeteria uses a hundred (loaf) _____ a day.

17. One's (belief) _____ change with maturity.

18. Their (summary) _____ were carefully written.

19. There were three (Harry) _____ in the physics class.

20. The (attorney) _____ presented convincing evidence.

Better Spelling

How did you do? If you had trouble, go back over the exercises. Also, don't forget that a dictionary is sometimes necessary to get the correct spelling! Use the spelling fix with any word that gives you trouble. The combined concentrated memory of the eyes, ears, and muscles is stronger than the power of forgetting.

By now you have undergone three important processes in learning how to spell plural endings.

1. You have studied the various rules covering plural endings.

2. You have seen examples of how the rules work for large groups of words.

3. You have used the rules yourself in various programs.

Exercise 3.24

Proofread the following paragraph for spelling errors. It is the same one that you proofread at the beginning of this lesson. For any line that contains an error, write the correct spelling in the blank provided. Note that some lines may be error-free.

1. _____ The reason why people follow normes

2. _____ is so that human societys will have

3. _____ some kind of order in them. Most

4. _____ people agree that norms are necessary,

5. _____ but some feel that it is unfair that

6. _____ there are different norms for a man

7. _____ than for a women. In fact most

8. _____ feminists believe that a revision of

9. _____ norm structure is one of the keyes to

10. _____ equality between the sexs. Yet sex

11. _____ forms are only one specie of

12. _____ discrimination against women. Women

13. _____ increasingly feel that they must protect

14. _____ themselfs from all social patterns and

15. _____ habits that degrade them, no matter

16. _____ what. While some sociologistes and

17. _____ psychologists are concerned about the

18. _____ future of the family unit, radical

19. _____ feminists claim that most culturs in

20. _____ the world have been divided in halfs for

21. _____ so long that the very idea of unity is a

22. _____ joke.

•••

3.4 Summary
•••

A. Rule for *ie* or *ei:*
Put *i* before *e*
Except after *c*
Or when sounded like *a*
As in *neighbor* and *weigh.*

B. Rule for doubling final consonants:
1. If a word with the accent on the last or only syllable
2. has a single final consonant that is
3. preceded by a single vowel,
4. then when adding a suffix beginning with a vowel
5. you *double* the final consonant.

C. Rules for forming plurals of nouns:
1. Most nouns are made plural simply by adding an *s*.
2. Words that end in *ss, sh, ch,* or *x* are made plural by adding *-es*.
3. Words ending in *y* preceded by a consonant are made plural by dropping the y and adding *-ies*. However, nouns ending in a *y* preceded by a vowel simply add an *s* to form the plural.
4. Most nouns that end in *f* or *fe* are made plural by adding an *s*. *Roof* becomes *roofs*, for example. Some such nouns, however, are made plural by changing the *f* to *v* and adding *s* or *-es*. *Wife* thus becomes *wives*, and <u>half</u> becomes *halves*.
5. Some nouns, such as *sheep*, keep the same spelling for both singular and plural.
6. Some old nouns in our language are made plural in unusual ways. *Goose* becomes *geese*, and *tooth* becomes *teeth*, for example.
7. Most nouns ending in *o* are made plural by adding an *s*. Thus, *halo* becomes *halos*. A few such nouns, however, take an *-es* in the plural; *cargo* becomes *cargoes*, for example.
8. Some nouns from Latin use the Latin form of the plural, as *alumnus, alumni*.

Exercise 3.25

Underline the correct spelling in 1-10. Check your work with the answers at the back of the book.

Example: The (cieling, <u>ceiling</u>) needs paint.

1. The three (thieves, theives) were captured at the scene of the crime.

2. They have ceased to use (monkies, monkeys) as subjects in the labs.

3. The doors to the auditorium (finaly, finally) opened to the ticket holders.

4. For thousands of years the tremendous (hieght, height) of the mountain passes made them inaccessible.

5. She wrote two volumes (detailing, detailling) the intricacies of numismatics.

6. In Fra Angelico's paintings the (haloes, halos) are gold.

7. All candidates will (recieve, receive) appropriate forms in the mail.

8. The most (compelling, compeling) views lie above the timber line.

9. The rural Russian (churches, churchs) and monasteries reveal the highest form of the art of wood joining.

10. You will have many (opportunitys, opportunities) to pursue the study of African languages on the graduate level.

Chapter 4

Words Commonly Confused

4.1 The Most Commonly Confused Words
• •

This section considers problems that can arise in spelling words that sound alike. We'll start with a diagnostic exercise to determine which words may be problematic for you.

Exercise 4.1

Proofread the paragraph for spelling errors, writing the correct spelling in the blanks provided. Not all lines will have errors. Check your answers before proceeding.

1. _____ Accept for its extreme aridity, the

2. _____ dessert would be a great place to live

3. _____ in. If you can get access to water,

4. _____ you're problems would be mostly

5. _____ over. The energy source is all ready

6. _____ there. Of coarse, I mean solar

7. _____ energy. It doesn't rain more then one

8. _____ day a year, on the average, in most

9. _____ desert areas, so you won't loose

10. _____ to much of the available energy from

11. _____ the sun. Just add a little technology and

12. _____ a lot of imagination to your water and

13. _____ energy supplies, and whose to say you

14. _____ couldn't build a paradise out there on

15. _____ the sandy planes?

If you were able to identify and spell correctly all the errors in the paragraph, skim the remainder of this chapter and go on to the next chapter, "Beginnings, Endings, and Apostrophes." Otherwise, stay with the programmed lessons that follow.

Now look closely at the misspellings in the paragraph. Did you notice something about them? What do they share in common? The misspellings were a result of confusion between words that sound alike but are spelled differently.

Let's begin by adding three more words to your spelling vocabulary: *homonym, homograph,* and *homophone.*

1. *Homonyms* are words that are spelled and pronounced alike but are different in meaning. A simple example of a homonym is the word *too.* This word can mean "excessively," as in "You are *too* late to get a ticket." (You could substitute the word *excessively* for *too* and the meaning of the sentence would not change.) But *too* can have another meaning: "also." "Tom is from Los Angeles, and Susan is from there *too.* " (You could substitute *also* for *too* and the sentence would still express the same idea.) There are many homonyms in the English language. Can you think of some others? Consider words such as *bill, loaf, foot,* and *ship.*

Since homonyms are spelled alike, they do not present a spelling problem as such, unless they are confused with still another word that is similar in sound.

2. *Homographs* are words that are spelled alike but are different in pronunciation and meaning. The noun *desert,* meaning "an arid, barren region," is spelled the same as the verb *desert,* which means "to withdraw from something" or "to abandon."

Let's look at the difference in pronunciation between the two words.

On which syllable does the accent fall in the noun meaning "an arid, barren region"?

_____

The first, *DESert*

On which syllable does the accent fall in the verb meaning "to withdraw from something"?

_____

The second, *deSERT*

Since these words, like homonyms, are spelled alike, they do not usually cause spelling problems unless they are confused with other similar-sounding words.

3. *Homophones* are words that are alike in pronunciation but are different in spelling and meaning. These are the really tricky words when it comes to spelling.

In the opening paragraph, six of the ten errors were made because of confusion between homophones. Can you name them?

1. _____   *you're* for *your*

2. _____   *all ready* for *already*

Better Spelling

3. _____   *coarse* for course

4. _____   *to* for *too*

5. _____   *whose* for *who's*

6. _____   *planes* for
                                                              plains

Now let's look at several pairs of homophones, including the six above, in order to see where errors might be made.

1. *It's—Its*

   It's is a contraction of *it* and *is*. The apostrophe is there to indicate the missing letter.

   Its is the possessive form of the pronoun *it*. *It* does not take an apostrophe in the possessive.

2. *You're—Your*

   You're is a contraction of *you* and *are,* hence the apostrophe.

   Your is the possessive form of the personal pronoun *you:* no apostrophe.

3. *All ready—Already*

   All ready is *two* words meaning "all are ready."

   Already is *one* word (and one *l*) meaning the same thing as *previously.*

4. *Their—There*

   Their is the possessive form of the pronoun *they:* no apostrophe!

   There means "that place."

   (Don't forget a third homophone *they're,* which is a contraction of *they* and *are.*)

5. *Coarse—Course*

   Coarse is a word meaning "rough."

Course refers to a path or a plan of study.

6. *To—Too*

To means "in the direction of." It is a preposition. *To* may also be followed by a verb to form the infinitive: *to run, to see.*

Too means either *excessively* or *also.*

(Don't forget a third homophone: the number *two.*)

7. *Whose—Who's*

Whose is the possessive form of the personal pronoun *who.* It takes no apostrophe.

Who's is a contraction of the words *who* and *is.*

8. *Planes—Plains*

Plane refers to flat surfaces or flying machines.

Plain refers to a flat, open region or to the quality of lacking ornamentation or beauty.

There is a fourth category of troublesome words closely related to homophones. They are not homophones because they are not pronounced alike when pronounced carefully and correctly, but in everyday speech we do not distinguish the differences in sound. They are "*pseudo*-homophones" or "near-homophones."

There is, for example, an error in the following sentence: "Offered money or love, I'll choose the later."

Where is the misspelling?	*later*
How should the word be spelled?	*latter*
How is the *a* pronounced in *latter?*	short *a* as in *hat*
How is the *a* pronounced in *later?*	long *a* as in *hate*

Can you find the errors in the opening paragraph that occurred as a result of confusion between pseudo-homophones? Write them down.

Better Spelling

1. _____   *accept* for *except*

2. _____   *dessert* for *desert*

3. _____   *then* for *than*

4. _____   *loose* for *lose*

Let's look at each one closely.

1. *Accept—Except*

   Accept means "to receive willingly," and it begins with an *a*, pronounced as in *hat*.

   Except means "other than," and it begins with an *ex*, with the *e* pronounced with a short *e* as in *bet*.

2. *Dessert—Desert*

   Dessert means "the last course in a meal," and the accent falls on the last syllable, *SERT*.

   Desert means "an arid, barren region," and the accent falls on the first syllable, *DES*. It also means "to leave," with the accent on the last syllable, *SERT*.

3. *Then—Than*

   Then means "at that time," and its vowel is pronounced as a short *e*, as in *her*.

   Than is used to express comparisons such as "other than" and "more than," and its vowel is a short *a* as in *man*.

4. *Loose—Lose*

   Loose means "free from attachment or restraint," and its *s* is aspirated, as in *bus*.

   Lose means "to misplace" or "to suffer defeat," and its *s* is pronounced as a *z (buzz)*.

4.1 The Most Commonly Confused Words

The following list contains groups of words that students commonly confuse and therefore frequently misspell. Sound them out and study them carefully.

Stare at the words, *pronounce* them by syllables, *engrave* them by writing them slowly and firmly, and *look* for *links*—associations that will remind you of the correct spellings.

affect — to have an influence on, used only as a verb
effect — result or consequence; as a verb, to cause a
    result

altar — a table in a place of worship
alter — to change

brake — to stop; a device for stopping
break — to separate into parts violently; the separation

capital — a major city; accumulated wealth; punishable
    by death
capitol — a building where legislative sessions are held

compliment — to praise
complement — to fill out or complete

council — a group meeting for a special purpose
counsel — to give advice

formally — conventionally; ceremoniously
formerly — previously

its — possessive form of it
it's — a contraction form of it is

lead — a heavy metal (pronounced *lĕd*); to direct or go
    before (pronounced *lēd*)
led — past tense of *to lead*

miner — one who works in a mine
minor — one below legal adulthood; unimportant

moral — good; a lesson in conduct
morale — mental spirit

passed — past tense of to pass
past — a previous time

peace — tranquility
piece — a part

personal — individual
personnel — people working in the same place

principal — headmaster of a school; most important
principle — a law or rule

quiet — silent
quite — very; somewhat, rather
quit — to stop or cease

stationary — fixed; still
stationery — paper used for writing

there — a place away from here
their — possessive form of they
they're — contraction of they are

threw — past tense of to throw
through — passing completely within

to — in the direction of; part of the infinitive of a verb:
   to run
too — excessively; also
two — the number

Now see how well you have mastered the correct spelling of the words on the list.

Exercise 4.2

Underline the correct spelling in the parentheses. Check your answers before proceeding.

1. The shortage of oil will (affect, effect) gasoline prices.

2. The earthquake (altared, altered) the river's course.

3. If you (brake, break) the glass, you have to buy it.

4. The (capital, capitol) city is the largest in the state.

5. The faculty (counsel, council) meets at noon.

6. Sri Lanka was (formally, formerly) called Ceylon.

7. (It's, Its) time to go to class.

8. The colonel (lead, led) the procession.

9. The accident caused a (minor, miner) delay.

10. The team's (morale, moral) was low after the loss.

11. We (passed, past) through Chicago on the way.

12. This (peace, piece) of music is for violin.

13. My (personal, personnel) feelings are private.

14. The (principal, principle) is retiring from the school.

15. It is always (quite, quiet) noisy in the lounge.

16. A box of new (stationary, stationery) has arrived.

17. If they miss the bus, (their, they're) going to be late.

18. She received many (complements, compliments) for her song.

19. He (through, threw) the used pages in the basket.

20. There are (two, too) many students in the class.

4.2 More Commonly Confused Words

Your writing teachers have been seeing many, many misspellings, and, instead of getting accustomed to some of them, they get all the more distressed. For years students have been warned that there are certain words that are often misspelled, and your writing teachers would like to feel that you have

Better Spelling

learned from the warning. As a consequence, when you misspell one of these, they probably heave unhappy sighs at the effort wasted. These words are common culprits in misspellings; if you can master them, you will have improved your writing a great deal. When you look at the words, remember that the keys to memorization are exercising your sense memories, repeating, and associating. We have, when possible, paired these words to help you see what association you must perceive. You have seen some of these words before in this book, but we want to repeat and reemphasize, so here is your second list of commonly confused words.

accept — to receive
except — everything other than

advice — what is received
advise — to tell what to do

aisle — a passage
isle — an island

already — before now
all ready — completed; prepared

alley — a narrow way
ally — a helper

altogether — entirely
all together — as a group; in unison

angel — celestial being
angle — a corner

baring — making bare
barring — obstructing
bearing — carrying

born — brought into being
borne — carried

breath — the air that goes in and out of the lungs
breathe — to move air in and out of the lungs

canvas — a cloth
canvass — to solicit

choose — the act of making a choice in the present
chose — having made a choice in the past

clothes — garments
cloths — pieces of cloth
close — to shut

conscience — an inner moral sense
conscious — aware

decent — honorable, respectable
descent — downward slope or motion
dissent — a disagreement, or to disagree

device — a piece of equipment
devise — to figure out a way

discreet — tactful
discrete — separate and distinct

dual — as in dual, or two, wheels
duel — a fight

holly — a tree
holy — hallowed, sacred
wholly — totally

hoping — wishing for or expecting something
hopping — jumping up and down

idea — a thought
ideal — a model of perfection

instance — an example
instants — periods of time

lessen — verb, to make less
lesson — noun, your study assignment

lose — to misplace
loose — not tight

Better Spelling

new — not used
knew — was aware of (past tense of *to know*)

nineteenth, ninetieth, and *ninety;* but *ninth*

no — opposite of *yes*
know — to be aware of

pail — a bucket
pale — lacking color; ashen

pair — a set of two
pear — a fruit
pare — to peel

patients — a doctor's clients
patience — willingness to wait

peer — someone's equal
pier — a wharf or jetty

precede — to come before
proceed — to continue or to move on

presence — state of being present
presents — gifts

right — okay
rite — ceremony
write — by hand or typewriter

scraped — chafed or rubbed
scrapped — threw out or gave up on

shone — from *shine*
shown — from *show*

sight — view, spectacle
site — a plot of ground
cite — to use as evidence

steal — to take by theft
steel — strong metal

whose — possessive of *who*
who's — contraction of *who is*

your — belonging to *you*
you're — contraction of *you are*

Exercise 4.3

Underline the correctly spelled word in each set of parentheses. Check your answers before proceeding.

1. My (advise, advice) to you is to apply for the job.
2. The play is set on a desert (isle, aisle).
3. Canada is a good (ally, alley) of the United States.
4. Draw an acute (angle, angel).
5. James is (bearing, baring) a load of bricks.
6. The calf was (born, borne) at three in the morning.
7. (Breathe, Breath) the fresh air deeply.
8. The tent is made of (canvas, canvass).
9. Wear warm (cloths, clothes) when you go skiing.
10. He was (unconscience, unconscious) for five minutes.

Exercise 4.4

Underline the correctly spelled word in each set of parentheses. Check your answers.

1. The trigger (devise, device) is broken.
2. He is a very (descent, decent) man.
3. The car has a (duel, dual) exhaust system.
4. He is (forty, fourty) years old today.

5. They have a high (regard, reguard) for Vanessa.
6. The (holly, wholly) tree has red berries.
7. The bird (hoped, hopped) across the path.
8. We waited several (instance, instants) before running.

Exercise 4.5

Underline the correctly spelled word in each set of parentheses. Check your answers.

1. Study the Spanish (lessen, lesson) well.
2. It is her (nineteenth, ninteenth) birthday.
3. The child's (presents, presence) was pleasing.
4. Religious (rites, rights) are held in every country.
5. He (scrapped, scraped) mud off his boots.
6. This is the (site, sight) for the new dotre.

Exercise 4.6

Underline the correctly spelled words in the parentheses. Check your answers.

1. Each professor must (advise, advice) ten students.
2. The central (isle, aisle) of the auditorium must be kept clear of spectators.
3. The shop is located in a small (ally, alley) between two department stores.
4. You must (device, devise) a way to combine the two chemicals.
5. The (descent, decent) from Mt. Durma was treacherously steep.

6. The college has always held the honors program in the highest (reguard, regard).

7. Yom Kippur is a (holy, holly) day.

8. Dance (lessens, lessons) are held on Thursday mornings.

Exercise 4.7

To complete this section, try your hand again at the paragraph that began the chapter. Proofread the paragraph for spelling errors. Put in your correction for any line containing an error in the blank provided. Note that some lines may be error-free. Check your answers.

1. _____ Accept for its extreme aridity, the

2. _____ dessert would be a great place to live

3. _____ in. If you can get access to water,

4. _____ you're problems would be mostly

5. _____ over. The energy source is all ready

6. _____ there. Of coarse, I mean solar

7. _____ energy. It doesn't rain more then one

8. _____ day a year, on the average, in most

9. _____ desert areas, so you won't loose

10. _____ to much of the available energy from

11. _____ the sun. Just add a little technology and

12. _____ a lot of imagination to your water and

13. _____ energy supplies, and whose to say you

14. _____ couldn't build a paradise out there on

15. _____ the sandy planes?

4.3 Summary

A. Homonyms are words that are spelled and pronounced alike but are different in meaning. The word *too* is a homonym. It has two very different meanings: "excessively" or "also."

B. Homographs are words that are spelled alike but are different in both pronunciation and meaning; For example, *desert,* with the accent on the first syllable, means "an arid, barren region." But *desert,* with the accent on the second syllable, is a verb meaning "to withdraw from something."

C. Homophones are words that sound alike but are different in both spelling and meaning. They are frequently misspelled. *Their, they're,* and *there* are examples of a homophone.

D. Pseudo-homophones, or near-homophones, are words that are pronounced nearly alike but are very different in both spelling and meaning. *Then* and *than* fall into this category of troublesome spelling words.

Exercise 4.8

Underline the correct spellings in 1-5. Check your work with the answers at the back of the book.

Example: (There, They're) here at last.

1. The (alter, altar) is in the front of the church.

2. The Sherpa guide (led, lead) the expedition through the mountain pass.

3. The armistice guaranteed them a sizable (piece, peace) of what was formerly enemy territory.

4. The heavily armed vehicle rolled slowly (passed, past) the hospital building and stopped.

5. If (it's, its) second-story windows could be opened, the building could be aired out in an hour.

Chapter 5

Beginnings, Endings, and Apostrophes

• •
5.1 Spelling Words with Prefixes, Suffixes, and Apostrophes
• •

Students frequently have problems spelling words with prefixes, suffixes, and apostrophes. We will begin with a diagnostic exercise to determine which words you may have problems with.

Exercise 5.1

Proofread the paragraph for spelling errors, writing the correct spelling in the blank provided. Note that some lines may be error-free. Check your answers before proceeding.

1. _____ Many students are disatisfied with the

2. _____ housing policies in the university. For

3. _____ one thing, they would like to have

4. _____ more say in the assigning of roomates.

Better Spelling

5. _____ It is completly

6. _____ unecessary, they argue, to make an

7. _____ arbitrary decision as to who will live

8. _____ with whom. But it is a diservice to

9. _____ attack the housing office without

10. _____ looking closly at its problems in recent

11. _____ years. First, most students wish to live

12. _____ on campus and are dissappointed if

13. _____ rooms are not available. Secondly, the

14. _____ enrolement has grown considerably in

15. _____ the last five years. Finaly, there is only

16. _____ limited space in the city campus for the

17. _____ university to build new dorms. The job

18. _____ of the housing office is realy like

19. _____ putting together a gigantic jigsaw

20. _____ puzzle with too many pieces to fit in

21. _____ the available spaces.

If you were able to identify and correctly spell the errors in the paragraph, skim the remainder of this chapter and go on to the next chapter, "Phonics." Otherwise, complete the following programmed lessons.

If you check with the answer key again, you will notice that the misspellings in the paragraph are the result of omitting or adding a letter. Students usually make such errors of omission or addition when spelling words that have prefixes (beginnings) and suffixes (endings). These are the two kinds of affixes, or "parts that attach."

5.1 Spelling Words with Prefixes, Suffixes, and Apostrophes

What is the prefix for the word *illegal*? _____
il

What is the suffix in the word *legally*? _____
ly

So, *legal* can have a prefix or a suffix. Can it have both? _____
yes, illegally

Does the spelling of *legal* change when you add a prefix? _____
no

In fact, the spelling of a word never changes when you add a prefix to it. Remember this rule. Even when the first letter of the word and the last letter of its prefix are the same, you still do not change the spelling.

Now practice this rule by adding prefixes to the following words:

1. mis + step = _____   misstep

2. co + operate = _____   cooperate

3. pre + eminent = _____   preeminent

4. un + necessary = _____   unnecessary

Remember not to *add* unnecessary letters:

5. dis + appoint = _____   disappoint

6. dis + appear = _____   disappear

7. un + interested = _____   uninterested

8. un + involved = _____   uninvolved

9. de + regulated = _____   deregulated

10. mis + fit = _____   misfit

Exercise 5.2

Underline the correct spelling in the parentheses. Check your answers before proceeding.

1. un + needed = (uneeded, unneeded)

2. pre + arranged = (preearranged, prearranged)

3. dis + satisfied = (dissatisfied, disatisfied)

4. mis + understand = (missunderstand, misunderstand)

5. re + enforce = (reenforce, renforce)

6. re + locate = (rellocate, relocate)

7. co + ordinate = (coordinate, cordinate)

8. dis + member = (dissmember, dismember)

9. re + place = (replace, repplace)

10. mis + spell = (mispell, misspell)

The same is usually true when you add a suffix to a word: The spelling stays the same.

enroll + ment =	_____	enrollment
careful + ly =	_____	carefully
final + ly =	_____	finally
appall + ing =	_____	appalling

One exception to this was discussed in Chapter 3 in the rule for doubling final consonants. Do you remember it? Let's look at it again.

1. When a word is accented on its last syllable (or if it has only one syllable)

2. and if it ends in a single consonant following a single vowel, then

3. if the suffix begins with a vowel you double the final consonant.

Example: run + ing = run*n*ing

Example: excel + ed = excel*l*ed

Now, what about words that end in *y?* There is a rule for such words. Do you know it?

If a word ends in *y* preceded by a consonant, change the *y* to *i* before any suffix that begins with any letter other than *i.*

Try some of these:

1. carry + ed = _____   carried

2. merry + er = _____   merrier

3. contrary + ly = _____   contrarily

4. marry + ing = _____   marrying

5. happy + ly = _____   happily

6. funny + er = _____   funnier

7. levy + ed = _____   levied

8. worry + ing = _____   worrying

9. sorry + er = _____   sorrier

10. play + ed = _____   played

What do you do when adding suffixes to words that end in silent *e?* When you add a suffix to words ending in silent *e,* sometimes you drop the silent *e* and sometimes you keep it. A simple rule that you can memorize will help you to spell most words in this category.

Better Spelling

Drop the final *e* when the suffix begins with a vowel, and keep the silent *e* when the suffix begins with a consonant.

Try some of these:

1. measure + ing = _____ measuring
2. leisure + ly = _____ leisurely
3. late + *n*ess = _____ lateness
4. value + able = _____ valuable
5. assure + ed = _____ assured
6. care + ing = _____ caring
7. polite + *n*ess = _____ politeness
8. aspire + ing = _____ aspiring
9. purple + ish = _____ purplish
10. negative + ity = _____ negativity

When the *e* is immediately preceded by another vowel, except *e*, it is often dropped from the derivative, *due, duly; argue, argument; true, truly; blue, bluish.* Fix on these spellings; they are tricky. Also note number 4 in the preceding list.

Exercise 5.3

Underline the correct spelling in the parentheses. Check your answers before proceeding.

1. rue + ing = (ruing, rueing)
2. argue + ment = (argument, arguement)
3. due + ly = (duely, duly)
4. true + ly = (truly, truely)
5. blue + ish = (bluish, blueish)

There are some troublesome words that end in silent *e*. Watch out for words that end in silent *e* preceded by a soft *g* or *c* as in *manage* and *notice*. These words *keep* the final *e* if the following suffixes begin with *a* or *o*.

Try some of these:

1. manage + able = _____ manageable

2. notice + able = _____ noticeable

3. office + ious = _____ officious

4. outrage + ous = _____ outrageous

5. courage + ous = _____ courageous

Exercise 5.4

Underline the correct spelling in these pairs. Check your answers before proceeding.

1. traceable, tracable

2. producable, produceable

3. manageing, managing

4. effacable, effaceable (from the word *efface*)

5. influential, influenteial

Exercise 5.5

Give the correct spelling of these combinations. Check your answers before proceeding.

1. propel + ed = _____

Better Spelling

2. care + ful = _____

3. ritual + ly = _____

4. marriage + able = _____

5. re + examine = _____

6. rescue + ing = _____

7. un + needed = _____

8. fulfill + ment = _____

9. manage + able = _____

10. hurry + ed = _____

11. im+ press = _____

12. salvage + able = _____

13. employ + er = _____

14. pro + fess = _____

15. confide + ing = _____

16. manual + ly = _____

17. forage + ing = _____

18. im+ material = _____

19. story + s = _____

20. storey + s = _____

Note: Compound words made up of two or more simple words usually retain all the letters: *well-bred, dull-eyed; save-all; wide-mouthed*. As time passes, some such words become known as one word, and a letter may be dropped: *almost, already, altogether, always, welfare, rueful, awful, pastime,* and *wherever*. It is still *all right;* it is still *all wrong*. It is not *alright*.

Exercise 5.6

Try these combinations. Check your answers before proceeding.

1. taste + full = _____
2. resent + full = _____
3. all + though = _____
4. all + so = _____
5. art + full = _____
6. all + mighty = _____
7. hate + full = _____
8. peace + full = _____
9. all + one = _____
10. well + come = _____

There is little explanation for how the words in the previous exercise were formed, and they are often misspelled. Avoid trouble by fixing on the correct spelling.

In considering the endings and beginnings of words, it is important to see how apostrophes are used.

Apostrophes are most commonly used to show where a letter has been dropped in joining two words together in a *contraction*. Also, they are sometimes used to show possession. Hundreds of years ago the correct spelling of a possessive ending in English was *es*. That spelling is no longer used, as the apostrophe has taken the place of the *e*.

Exercise 5.7

Proofread for spelling errors involving the lack of or misuse of apostrophes. Write in the correct spelling for any line containing

Better Spelling

an error in the blank provided. Note that some lines may be error-free. Check your answers before proceeding.

1. _____ It is unfair if a professors grading

2. _____ standards vary very much from the

3. _____ norm of the college. Of course there

4. _____ has to be some variation, but if

5. _____ Professor Hess's standards are much

6. _____ higher than those of Professor Jones,

7. _____ then there is a problem. College

8. _____ freshmens attitudes toward learning can

9. _____ be tainted by such a situation and the

10. _____ student's confidence in their professors

11. _____ is sure to diminish. Some students feel

12. _____ powerless to change unfair grading

13. _____ policies while others feel that it is the

14. _____ faculty's responsibility to change the

15. _____ policies, not their's. In reality it is

16. _____ everyones responsibility. It

17. _____ doesnt matter how many

18. _____ As or Fs are given in a department

19. _____ as much as whether or not the

20. _____ grading is consistent.

If you made more than one error, you need to work on this lesson on apostrophes.

The rules for using apostrophes are fairly simple and consistent. You can avoid errors of this type by learning the following points.

1. Form the possessive of most singular nouns by adding an apostrophe and an *s*.

Example: the notes of the teacher — the teacher's notes

Example: the property of the woman — the woman's property

Exercise 5.8

Form the possessives below. Check your answers before proceeding.

1. the books belonging to Tom — Tom_____ books

2. the tail of the dog — the dog_____ tail

3. the height of the tower — the tower_____ height

4. the roots of the tree — the tree_____ roots

5. the life of Marie — Marie_____ life

2. For words of two or more syllables that end in *s*, form the possessive by adding an apostrophe (do not add an *s*). Monosyllabic words that end in *s* take an apostrophe and an *s* to form the possessive.

Example: the charm of the hostess — the hostess' charm

Example: the results of the process — the process' results

Example: the desk of the boss — the boss's desk

Exercise 5.9

Try these possessive-apostrophe forms. Check our answers before proceeding.

1. the springs of the mattress — the mattress____ springs
2. the stripes of the lioness — the lioness____ stripes
3. the tires of the bus — the bus____ tires
4. the shape of the glass — the glass____ shape
5. the beard of his highness — his highness____ beard

3. For plural nouns that do not end in s, form the plural by adding an apostrophe and an s.

Example: the dorm of the men — the men's dorm

Example: literature for children — children's literature

Exercise 5.10

Fill in the blanks with the correct possessive forms. Check your answers.

1. the group of the women — the women____ group
2. the bulk of the oxen — the oxen____ bulk
3. the hole of the mice — the mice____ hole
4. the wings of the lice — the lice____ wings
5. the honking of the geese — the geese____ honking

4. Form the possessive of a plural noun ending in *s* by adding an apostrophe (do not add an *s*).

Example: the offices of the administrators- — the administrators' offices

Example: the uniforms of the players — the players' uniforms

Exercise 5.11

Try these possessive forms. Check your answers.

1. the union of the actors — the actor_____ union

2. the decision of the judges — the judge _____ decision

3. the dorms of the students — the student_____ dorms

4. the photograph of the wives — the wives_____ photograph

5. the works of the painters — the painter_____ works

5. Personal pronouns in the possessive (*his, hers, its, ours, yours, theirs, whose*) do not take an apostrophe.

Example: these are her books — these books are hers

Exercise 5.12

Fill in the blanks below to complete the correct possessive forms.

1. the footprints belonging to it — it_____ footprints

2. our books — the books are our_____

Better Spelling

3. your house — the house is your_____
4. their belongings — the belongings are their_____
5. the books belonging to whom — who_____ books

6. Indefinite pronouns, such as *one, everybody,* and *everyone* form the possessive by taking an apostrophe and an *s.*

Example: the responsibility of everyone — everyone's responsibility

Example: in the best interest of one — in one's best interest

---

Exercise 5.13

Fill in the blanks below.

1. the fault of somebody — somebody_____ fault
2. the job of someone — someone_____ job
3. the interest of everybody — everybody_____ interest
4. the task of one — one_____ task
5. the time of everyone — everyone_____ time

A contraction is one word made up of two words. For example, "aren't" is a contraction of the words "are" and "not."

7. When a letter is omitted in a contraction, use an apostrophe to show the place where the letter or letters have been removed.

Example: It is not difficult — It isn't difficult.

Example: Do not fail the test — Don't fail the test.

102

Exercise 5.14

Make the following contractions.

1. must + not = _____

2. will + not = _____

3. they + will = _____

4. we + are = _____

5. it + is = _____

8. To avoid confusion, it is often wise to make the plural form of a letter or number by adding an apostrophe and an *s*. Style guides vary on this matter, but generally either using or omitting the apostrophe will be acceptable in your college papers.

Example: I got an A in English and math—I got two A's (rather than *two As*).

Exercise 5.15

Try these number and letter plurals.

1. one *n* plus another *n* — two *n*_____

2. an 85 in French and an 85 in Math — two 85_____

3. a C in Science and a C in History — two C_____

4. a 3.5 in both semesters — two 3.5_____

5. *Middle* has two *d*_____

9. When two coordinate nouns share a common possessive, only the second noun takes an apostrophe and an *s*.

Example: the project of Tom and Bill — Tom and Bill's project.

10. When two coordinate nouns show possession separately, both nouns take an apostrophe and an *s*.

Example: the physics books of Tom and Bill — Tom's and Bill's physics books

---

Exercise 5.16

Write the possessive forms of the following coordinate nouns. Use *'s* only where necessary.

1. the project of Tom, Bill, and Jean — Tom____, Bill____, and Jean____ project

2. the company of Mason and Firth — Mason____and Firth____company

3. the houses of Ann and Mary — Ann____ and Mary____ houses

4. the legs of John and Sam — John____ and Sam____ legs

5. the party of Sue and Peter — Sue____ and Peter____ party

Exercise 5.17

Here is the paragraph that you proofread at the beginning of the lesson. Proofread it again, using the rules governing apostrophes. If you have trouble with a word, find the appropriate rule to see how to use the apostrophe correctly. For every line containing an error, write the correct spelling in the blank provided. Note that some lines may be error-free.

1. _____ It is unfair if a professors grading
2. _____ standards vary very much from the
3. _____ norm of the college. Of course there
4. _____ has to be some variation, but if
5. _____ Professor Hess's standards are much
6. _____ higher than those of Professor Jones,
7. _____ then there is a problem. College
8. _____ freshmens attitudes toward learning can
9. _____ be tainted by such a situation and the
10. _____ student's confidence in their professors
11. _____ is sure to diminish. Some students feel
12. _____ powerless to change unfair grading
13. _____ policies while others feel that it is the
14. _____ faculty's ponsibility to change the
15. _____ policies, not their's. In reality it is
16. _____ everyones responsibility. It
17. _____ doesnt matter how many
18. _____ As or Fs are given in a department
19. _____ as much as whether or not the
20. _____ grading is consistent.

5.2 Summary

A. The spelling of a word never changes when you add a prefix to it. *Co* and *ordinate* make *coordinate.*

B. The spelling of a word usually stays the same if you add a suffix. *Careful* plus *ly* make *carefully.*

C. There are times, however, when the spelling of a word changes when a suffix is added.

   1. Remember the rule for doubling final consonants in Chapter 3? *If a word is accented on the last or only syllable, and if it ends in a single consonant following a single vowel, then double the consonant in adding a suffix beginning with a vowel. Run* plus *ing* become *running,* and *propel* plus *er* make *propeller.*

   2. Also, *if a word ends in y preceded by a consonant, change the y to i before adding a suffix that begins with any letter other than i.* Thus, *contrary* plus *ly* become *contrarily,* and *merry* plus *er* become *merrier,* but it's *marrying.*

   3. Most of the time you *drop the final silent e when it is followed by a suffix beginning with a vowel, and keep the final silent e when it is followed by a suffix beginning with a consonant.* So *value* plus *able* become *valuable,* and *leisure* plus *ly* make *leisurely.*

   4. Words that end in silent e *preceded by a soft g or c keep the final e before suffixes beginning with a or o.* Thus, *courage* plus *ous* become *courageous* and *notice* plus *able* make *noticeable.*

D. The rules for apostrophes are simple and consistent.

1. Apostrophes are used in various ways to show the possession of nouns: singular: *woman's pocketbook*
singular of two or more syllables ending in *s: hostess' charm* but *boss's decision*
plural not ending in *s: women's pocketbook*
plural ending in *s: administrators' offices*
common possession: *Bill and Tom's dog*
separate possession: *Britain's and America's navies*

2. Personal pronouns such as his and theirs do not take apostrophes in the possessive form, but indefinite pronouns such as *someone* and *everyone* do: *someone's, everyone's.*

3. An apostrophe is used to show where a letter has been removed in forming a contraction. *Does* plus *not* become *doesn't.*

4. Plurals of letters or numbers are formed with an apostrophe and an *s.* Examples: *90's, a's.*

Exercise 5.18

Underline the correct spelling in the parentheses. Check the answers at the back of the book.

Example: It is (<u>illegal</u>, ilegal) to hunt at this time of year.

1. It would have been a great (dissappointment, disappointment) not to have qualified.

2. The responsibility is (their's, theirs).

3. The curriculum is (manageable, managable) if you work very hard.

4. (One's, Ones) first responsibility is to maintain the survival of the group.

---

5. Chapter 9 is (making, makeing) more sense now.
6. The Language Department (does'nt, doesn't) offer that class anymore.
7. She's (running, runing) for representative.
8. The (womens', women's) group meets on Thursdays after work.
9. The children are (happyer, happier) now that the playground is finished.
10. The (hostess's, hostess') charm assured the success of the evening.

Chapter 6
Phonics

6.1 Phonics and Spelling

As you learned in Chapter 2, the study of phonics is the study of the sounds of language. In this chapter, we will be discussing different aspects of phonics. We'll begin with a diagnostic exercise to see where you may have problems.

Exercise 6.1

Proofread the paragraph for spelling errors, writing the correct spelling in the blank provided. Check your answers before proceeding. Note that some lines may be error-free.

1. _____ It is extreamly important to

2. _____ preform the calculations correctly. A

3. _____ mistake would be disasterous. Each

4. _____ scientist must call upon the greatest

5. _____ skill he has. Personal conveience must

6. _____ be forgotten, for each person may have

7. _____ to work at his computer for at least

8. _____ five hours straight. Since all are mili-

9. _____ tary personnel, they must acomadate

10. _____ the commanding officer and do what

11. _____ they are ordered to do. On occaision

12. _____ one may request a rest period, but the

13. _____ goverment regulations are strict in this

14. _____ regard. Sucess in producing the final

15. _____ equation will benifit everyone,

16. _____ but an error could bring about a

17. _____ national tradgedy.

If you made no more than one mistake, skim this chapter and go on to the next. If you made more than one error, you need to read this chapter on phonics carefully.

This chapter not only discusses aspects of *phonics* but also reviews the spelling fix. These words can be spelled correctly if you develop a special pronunciation pattern for each one that aids the spelling memory. Each word is to be broken down into simple syllables that indicate the correct spelling and pronunciation.

Look, for example, at the noun *pronunciation*. This word appears on many lists of demons (frequently misspelled words) in spelling books. The error usually occurs in the second syllable, which is usually misspelled by adding an *o* before the *u*. Now, using the dictionary, break the word into sound groups that will help you both spell and pronounce it correctly. The syllabic spelling is:

pro-*nun*-ci-a-tion

You can see that the second syllable is spelled and sounded differently from the second syllable in pro-*nounce*. Confusion between these two syllables usually causes the error.

By carefully and slowly *sounding* and then *writing* out the correct letter groups according to the syllable pattern given in the dictionary, you can reinforce the correct spelling in your memory. When you use this word in your own writing, sound it and write it out carefully and slowly, concentrating on each syllable sound as you write. This is, of course, part of the spelling fix. Chances are very good that the next time you use the word, you will remember the syllable pattern and spell the word correctly.

It has taken a lot of words to show how this memory technique works for just one word, *pronunciation*. Once you see how it works, however, the technique is simple. Now see how it works for other words.

1. *accurate*

   ac-cu-rate

   This word is usually misspelled by omitting one of the *c's*. If you *sound out* and then *write* each syllable separately, you will not misspell it. If you have trouble with the last syllable, exaggerate the syllable, even giving it the long $\bar{a}$ sound as in the word *rate,* so that you will remember the correct spelling.

2. *extremely*

   ex-treme-ly

   Here the error usually occurs in the second syllable. You can break the sound down even further to *trem-e* to help you remember the spelling pronunciation.

3. *together*

   to-geth-er

   No *a* after the *e* in the second syllable! Just a short *e* sound. Don't confuse this word with *heather* or *weather*. Fix the correct spelling in your mind.

4. *possesses*

   pos-ses-ses

   That's right! There are five *s*'s in this word. Note that the last two syllables are identical: *ses*.

5. *tomorrow*

   to-mor-row

   This shows you clearly, right from the dictionary, that this word has only one *m* and two *r*'s, not vice versa. Pronounce it this way whenever you write it.

6. *habit*

   hab-it

   Only one *b*. Sound it out that way when you spell it on paper.

7. *convenience*

   con-ve-nience

   You can even say the third syllable as two: *ni-ence*. Write it, using these syllable sounds.

8. *necessity*

   ne-ces-si-ty

   As you can see from reading and saying the second and third syllables, this word has one *c* and two *s*'s, not vice versa.

9. *similar*

   sim-i-lar

   As the dictionary shows, there is no *i* in the last syllable. Don't confuse this word with "familiar," which *does* end in *-iar*.

10. *occurred*

oc-curred

Here you may break the second syllable down even further, *cur-red,* to give the fullest spelling pronunciation.

Exercise 6.2

Underline the correct spelling in these pairs. Check your answers before proceeding.

1. acurrate, accurate
2. extreamly, extremely
3. together, togeather
4. posesses, possesses
5. tomorrow, tommorow

6. habbit, habit
7. convenience, convience
8. neccessity, necessity
9. similiar, similar
10. occurred, ocured

Do you see how this part of the spelling fix can point the way to correct spelling? Now try your hand at it.

Exercise 6.3

Write the correct syllable patterns for the next ten words. If necessary, use your dictionary to find them.

1. amount _____
2. business _____
3. occasion_____
4. success _____
5. performed_____

6. describe _____
7. government_____
8. practical _____
9. acquaint _____
10. professor _____

Exercise 6.4

Underline the correct spelling in the following pairs.

1. amount, ammount
2. buisness, business
3. occassion, occasion
4. sucess, success
5. performed, preformed
6. discribe, describe
7. government, goverment
8. practicle, practical
9. aquaint, acquaint
10. proffessor, professor

Note: In basketball, good shooters say that they often know if a shot is going to go in or not as soon as the ball leaves their fingers. In the case of a missed shot, they would say "something *felt* wrong." The same can be true of spelling. When you learn a word, learn also what it *feels* like to write it correctly. Feel the spelling syllables flow through the muscles in your hand that holds the pen. When you become sensitive to correct spelling, you can almost *feel,* through the memory of your eyes and muscles, when you have spelled the word correctly. You will have it engraved in your memory.

Students who write with little or no attention to the physical process of writing are likely to make more "careless" spelling errors than do those who are attuned to the *feel* of correct spelling. Using the S-P-E-L-L spelling fix works for "outlaws," words commonly confused, words governed by specific rules, or, indeed, *any* kind of spelling.

As you sound a word out according to the phonic spelling given in the dictionary, *exaggerate* the sound of the separate syllables. Say the word aloud several times using this exaggerated pronunciation.

BEN-E-FIT
GOV-ERN-MENT
AC-COM-MO-DATE

This will help you to include all the right letters and none of the wrong ones when you spell such words.

Exercise 6.5

Thinking about the correct phonics of the words below, say the words by syllables and underline the correct spelling in each pair. Check your answers before you proceed.

1. disasterous, disastrous
2. accomodate, accommodate
3. dependent, dependant
4. relavant, relevant
5. benefit, benlilt

6. irresistable, irresistible
7. indispensible, indispensable
8. tradgedy, tragedy
9. inventor, inventer
10. jewelor, jeweler

Exercise 6.6

Now, using your dictionary when necessary, look up the following words and write (carefully) the spelling pronunciations according to syllable patterns.

1. opportunity _____
2. curriculum _____
3. warrant _____
4. across _____
5. image _____

6. exaggerate _____
7. separate _____
8. ordered _____
9. explanation _____
10. comfortable _____

Better Spelling

Now that you have seen and written these words by syllables, block off the preceding list and underline the correctly
spelled words in the following pairs.

1. opportunity, oppertunity   6. exagerrate, exaggerate

2. curicculum, curriculum   7. seperate, separate

3. warrent, warrant   8. ordered, ordred

4. accross, across   9. explanation, explainaton

5. image, immage   10. comfortable, confortable

Now that you have learned how phonics can be an aid to better spelling and pronunciation and have tried the spelling fix
by using the combined memories of eyes, ears, and muscles,
try one last test and memory reinforcer.

Exercise 6.8

Here is the same paragraph that you proofread at the beginning of this chapter. Proofread the paragraph for spelling
errors again, writing the correct spelling in the blank provided. Note that some lines may be error-free.

1. _____ It is extreamly important to

2. _____ preform the calculations correctly. A

3. _____ mistake would be disasterous. Each

4. _____ scientist must call upon the greatest

5. _____ skill he has. Personal conveience must

6. _____ be forgotten, for each person may have

7. _____ to work at his computer for at least

8. _____ five hours straight. Since all are mili-

9. _____ tary personnel, they must acomadate

10. _____ the commanding officer and do what

11. _____ they are ordered to do. On occaision

12. _____ one may request a rest period, but the

13. _____ goverment regulations are strict in this

14. _____ regard. Sucess in producing the final

15. _____ equation will benifit everyone,

16. _____ but an error could bring about a

17. _____ national tradgedy.

• •

6.2 Summary
• •

A. Many spelling errors are made because students mispronounce the words. To avoid such errors, students should learn the correct *phonic pronunciation* of a word.

B. A word that is a candidate for misspelling needs to be *broken down into its syllable pattern.* The dictionary can give you the correct syllabification of such a word.

C. Then the word is locked in memory by *pronouncing each syllable in an exaggerated way, by writing the word in its correct form, syllable by syllable, and by seeing the correct sequence of syllables.* This process of coordinating the ear, hand, and eye muscles is called the spelling fix. It sensitizes students to the correct *feel* of a word through the senses of sound, touch, and sight.

Better Spelling

Underline the correct spelling in the parentheses. Check your work with the answers at the back of the book.

Example: The play was a (<u>tragedy</u>, tradegy).

1. The (personell, personnel) department must review all of the résumés.

2. The (pronunciation, pronounciation) of romance languages is rather difficult.

3. The student services committee will make every effort to (accommodate, accomadate) the Asian students.

4. I have had (ocassion, occasion) to use that word in every paragraph.

5. A (benifit, benefit) will be held on Friday night for the Youth Services staff.

6. It is difficult to (seperate, separate) fact from opinion in this essay.

7. Do not (exaggerate, exagerrate) your statistics.

8. Students who missed the exam will have an (opportunity, oppertunity) to make it up soon.

9. Registration for this year's election ends (tomorrow, tommorow).

10. The (government, goverment) has not responded to growing civil unrest in the rural areas.

Chapter 7
Outlaws

7.1 Spelling Outlaws

· ·

We use the term *outlaw* to describe a word the spelling of which appears to be random or arbitrary. Of course, there are no true outlaw words. All words have, to some extent, traceable histories that can help to explain their spelling. The study of the history of words is known as *etymology*.

This book is not a study of etymology, but you need to understand that language changes very gradually over the centuries. The language that was spoken in Britain a thousand years ago and from which modern English is in part derived would be incomprehensible to you. Very many of the words we use today and the general structure of our language grew out of that earlier speech. In addition, we retain some spelling conventions from spelling systems that existed earlier in our language's history, even though those spelling conventions do not appear to make sense. Consider the word *ghost*. Why is the *h* there? Originally the *h* had a function relating to pronunciation that no longer exists. But we still keep the *h* in *ghost*. Thus, lacking the history of the word, we have what we call an outlaw spelling.

Better Spelling

In the diagnostic exercises in Chapter 1 you encountered many outlaw words. We shall look closely at a number of them, considering methods that may be used to reinforce the correct spelling.

1. *incentive:* Here a *c* is used instead of an *s.* See if the word suggests a sound and spelling relationship that can be made into a "saying" for reinforcing the spelling. Here is an example: "In*cent*ive can earn you dollars and *cents.*" This is known as a mnemonic device, a trick to aid memory. Mnemonic devices can be very effective in mastering outlaw spellings.

2. *until:* Let's try a rhyme for this: "When you spell *until,* drop an *l,* if you will."

3. *whether:* The confusion here is both between the homonyms *whether* and *weather* and the presence of the *h* in *whether.* Try "*Wea*ther tells you what to *wear*" and "Use an *h whe*never you write *whe*ther" as mnemonic devices.

4. *exercise:* Here, in spelling the word exer*cise,* remember to be pre*cise.* When you write the word, remember the feeling and the look of the word as it is formed by your hand on the paper. The memory of a concentrated visual and muscular effort can be strong; it tends to stay "in the back of the mind." Concentrating on the spelling process in this fashion can be very helpful with outlaws.

5. *therefore:* Remember, "There are three *e*'s in there-fore," and "Both *there* and *their* start with *the.*"

6. *almost:* } When you add the prefix *all* to make an adverb, you drop an *l.*
7. *already:* } As a separate word, you keep both *l*'s: "*all*
8. *always:* } *wrong* or "*all right.*"

9. *dealt:* This is easy! To make the past tense of *deal,* just add a *t.*

10. *menu:* Some people want to add an *e* at the end of this word. "One *e* is enough for *menu.*"

Exercise 7.1

Underline the correctly spelled word in each pair. Check your answers before proceeding.

1. insentive, incentive	6. almost, allmost
2. until, untill	7. delt, dealt
3. whether, wether	8. menue, menu
4. presice, precise	9. allready, already
5. therefor, therefore	10. always, allways

Use the spelling fix whenever possible. If you combine a mnemonic device with concentration on the sight, sound, and feel of the actual writing process, you will reinforce the correct spelling of troublesome words.

Here are some ideas to remember about outlaws:

1. When in doubt about spelling an outlaw, use your dictionary. It will not let you down.

2. Keep a list of your own outlaw words. Use the list as a reference. If you use it carefully, eventually you will not need it.

3. When you write an outlaw on your "most wanted list" or elsewhere, concentrate on the visual and muscular feel of writing the word. This will help you to remember the correct spelling *experience.*

---

4. Use mnemonic devices such as those cited earlier. Make up your own, but keep them short, simple, and correct.

Now look at three more outlaws.

1. *develop:* "St*op* with the *p;* don't add an *e!*"

2. *instead:* "*Eat* bre*ad* inste*ad* of le*ad!*"

3. *ghost:* "Keep the *host* in *ghost!*"

Sometimes the catch-phrasing of such mnemonic devices borders on graffiti. Remember that they are most effective when kept simple and brief, such as the following:

1. There's *a rat* in sep*arat*e.

2. There's *iron* in the envi*ron*ment.

3. We're on the *edge* of knowl*edge*.

4. It's a privi*lege* to have *leg*s.

5. Don't forget to *add* your *add*ress.

6. *Emma* is my dil*emma*.

7. This is a desp*erate era*.

8. Ecst*asy* is e*asy*.

9. You can get to the c*emetery* with ease (*e*'s!).

10. *Ale* is prev*ale*nt here.

Exercise 7.2

See if you can remember the mnemonic devices for the ten preceding words. In this exercise, underline the correct spelling in each pair of words. Check your answers before proceeding.

1. seperate, separate
2. environment, enviroment
3. knowlege, knowledge
4. privilege, priviledge
5. adress, address
6. dilemma, dillema
7. desparate, desperate
8. ecstacy, ecstasy
9. cemetary, cemetery
10. prevelant, prevalent

7.2 Outlaw Forms

The choice between the endings -*ible* and -*able* is often confusing. There is an etymological explanation: -*ible* forms usually have come directly from the Latin *(sensible)*; the -*able* forms have usually been formed in English *(blamable, laudable)*. This is not very helpful. All you can do with these outlaws is to note that most forms have the -*able* ending. When you come across a word with -*ible,* use the spelling fix to lock the spelling into your mind.

The choice between *ensure* and *insure, enclose* and *inclose, enquire* and *inquire, incumbrance* and *encumbrance* also relates to the history of the words, with the *en-* form being the usual Latin spelling. Through the years the words have gradually changed to the point that, although both forms are acceptable, the *in-* form is preferred.

Words ending with -*ance* and -*ence* were once interchangeable, but now *dependent* and *dependence,* and *defendant, attendant, repentant* are preferred.

Some writers feel it adds glamor to their writing if they use British spellings. They do not go so far as to use *kerb* for *curb* or *tyre* for *tire,* but they write *humour* for *humor, colour* for *color, harbour* for *harbor,* and *glamour* for *glamor.* To most authorities this practice seems a prissy affectation; they suggest

Better Spelling

that when in Rome do as the Romans do; when writing in America, write as the Americans write. Americans now write *center* instead of *centre*, *meter* instead of *metre*; *theater* instead of *theatre*. *Acre, lucre, massacre,* and *ogre* retain the British forms. In New England some older forms persist in place names, for instance, Odeon *Theatre* and *Centre* Street.

The confusion about whether to end a word with *-ise* or *-ize* also is rooted in the past. Greek words tend to be ended with *-ize*, for instance, *anesthetize, baptize, characterize, dramatize, tantalize. Memorize* and *sensitize* are patterned after this form. If the word comes from a French verb, the *-ise* form is usually used: *apprise, comprise, enterprise, surprise.* Here again the practice is so inconsistent that you must recognize these words as troublemakers, and use the spelling fix on them. Some words to master are *advertise, advise, arise, chastise, circumcise, compromise, demise, despise, devise, disenfranchise, disguise, exercise, franchise, merchandise, premise, revise, supervise, surmise,* and *surprise.*

Exercise 7.3

See if you can remember the correct spelling of these words with outlaw beginnings or endings. Underline the correct or preferred American spelling in each pair. Check your answers before proceeding.

1. anesthetise, anesthetize
2. surprise, surprize
3. advertise, advertize
4. memorise, memorize
5. compromise, compromize
6. exercise, exercize
7. sensitize, sensitise
8. supervise, supervize

9. revise, revize
10. dependant, dependent
11. acer, acre
12. masssacre, massacer
13. attendent, attendant
14. defendent, defendant
15. inquire, enquire
16. ensure, insure

17. repentant, repentent	19. baptise, baptize
18. lucer, lucre	20. disguize, disguise

Another group of outlaw endings consists of those words that all end in the sound "seed," such as:

supersede   *exceed*   *concede*

These words are frequently misspelled. Here's how to keep them straight:

1. *Supersede* is the only word that ends in *sede.*

2. *Exceed, proceed,* and *succeed* are the only words that end in *ceed.*

3. All the rest end in *cede,* including *precede, recede,* and *secede.*

Exercise 7.4

See if you can remember the spellings of the outlaw words that end in the "seed" sound. Underline the correct spelling in each of these pairs. Check your answers before proceeding.

1. preceed, precede	6. cede, ceed
2. excede, exceed	7. proceed, procede
3. secede, seceed	8. conceed, concede
4. receed, recede	9. succeed, suceed
5. supersede, supercede	10. intercede, intersede

7.3 Silent Letter Outlaws

Another kind of outlaw word that gives writers trouble is the one with the silent letter. We suggest that you skim over the possible silent letter combinations and sensitize yourself to them:

gn, kn, pn for *n*	*pt, th, ght* for *t*	*wh* for *h*
rh, wr for *r*	*ps, sc* for *s*	

Exercise 7.5

Underline the silent letter(s). Check your answers before proceeding.

1. gneiss (a kind of rock)
2. knoll
3. Ptolemy (a Greek astronomer and mathematician)
4. wrestle
5. mnemonic
6. pneumonia
7. psalm
8. pseudonym
9. hymn
10. whole
11. height
12. sight
13. solemn
14. condemn

Exercise 7.6

What consonants are silent in these words? Underline the silent letters. Check your answers.

1. science	10. honest
2. rheumatism	11. honorable
3. wrist	12. heir
4. chlorine	13. wrong
5. gnu	14. gnome
6. ptomaine	15. muscle
7. solemn	16. rhyme
8. playwright	17. rhythm
9. writ	18. subtle

Exercise 7.7

Try this brief exercise on silent letter words. Add the missing silent letters in the blank spaces provided. Check your answers.

1. There is a grassy _____noll at the top of the slope.

2. The _____restling team was undefeated this winter.

3. Use _____nemonic devices to help you remember how to spell outlaws.

4. The _____hole campus was deserted during Christmas vacation.

5. At the hei____t of the festival, the sacred dances were performed.

6. The procession was solem____ and dignified.

7. The condem____ed prisoners still await a last-minute pardon from the governor.

8. The poem has a perfect r____yme pattern.

9. There is a su____tle difference between their religious philosophies.

10. ____neumonia can now be treated with antibiotics.

7.4 Four Esoteric Outlaws

The word esoteric means "known only to a few," and it is a term that applies, unhappily, to the spelling of the next words to be discussed.

Occasionally in newspapers you may see the expression "to the manor born," which seems to make sense. It could well describe a person born in a mansion or manor of the wealthy; it could mean accustomed to the practices of high or polite society. The correct spelling and meaning, however, comes from the expression in Shakespeare's *Hamlet*, "... though I am a native here/And to the manner born—it is a custom/More honor'd in the breach than the observance." This expression is the one often used to show life-long familiarity with certain elite customs or conditions. Thus, a euphemistic or tactful way of saying that a person was poor when born would be to say he was not to the manner born.

There are reasons for spelling that are too rarely known. As second example is the complex adjective, made out of two or more words. The question is when the words should be connected by hyphens, and not many people know. The convention is that if the modifier comes before the modified word, it is hyphenated; if it comes after the word, it is not hyphenated. In the following examples the modifier is underlined once; the word modified is underlined twice.

First-rate products will sell well.

The product is first rate.

A second-class citizen really is burdened with problems.

That citizen is second class.

That was an awe-inspiring production.

The production was awe inspiring.

That day remains in my memory as a never-to-be-forgotten experience.

The experience was never to be forgotten.

Yet another common confusion is caused by the word hang. What we usually see is this series of tenses:

Tom hangs his hat on the hook.

Yesterday Tom hung his hat on the hook.

In his years at work he has hung his hat on the hook many times.

When the expression refers to capital punishment, use a different past tense and past participle.

He is a stern judge; he hangs more convicted prisoners than he imprisons.

Frontier courts hanged cattle rustlers on the flimsiest of evidence.

Better Spelling

Some Western horse thieves have been hanged without a jury trial.

The word *accommodate,* which has been discussed before in this text, should be mentioned here. It is a word that professional writers misspell frequently. It should have two *c*'s and two *m*'s. The next time you see the word in the newspaper check to see if the reporter knew how to spell it.

Exercise 7.8

To check your knowledge of how to spell esoteric words and expressions, do this exercise. Proofread the paragraph and underline the correct spellings in the parentheses.

1. _____ Tom's knowledge of history is (awe-inspiring, awe inspiring),

2. _____ and his (first-rate, first rate) performance in "Fraternity Follies" was hilarious. But

3. _____ when he (hung, hanged) his soiled laundry over the balcony railing, his image took a nose dive. Can't he

4. _____ (accomodate, accommodate) himself to the values of the rest of us in the house? He was certainly not, as

5. _____ the English would say, to the (manor, manner) born!

7.5 Thirty of the Hardest Outlaws in English

Another list of words that may help you is taken from one prepared by the Word Guild, an international consortium of freelance editors and writers. To help professional writers catch words likely to end up misspelled on the printed page, the Guild assembled a list for them to tack up in front of their desks. The list has undoubtedly prevented much embarrassment.

These are thirty of the words found misspelled most frequently in print.

accordion	incidentally
analyze	indispensable
annihilate	innocuous
bureau	inoculate
commitment	irresistible
committee	liaison
consensus	mischievous
descendant	occurrence
desperate (moved by despair)	permissible
ecstasy	precede
guerrilla	quandary
harass	rhythm
hypocrisy	saxophone
idiosyncrasy	stratagem
incalculable	superintendent

Better Spelling

To fix each of these words in your mind, use the S-P-E-L-L technique. Using this multisensory approach can you help to place such difficult words in your permanent spelling memory. It would be helpful for you to review the SPELL technique at this point before attempting the exercise on the "most frequently misspelled words."

Read what each of the letters in the SPELL acronym stands for:

S *S*tare at the word. Accustom your "eye memory" to the way the word looks in print.

P *P*ronounce the word. Exaggerate each syllable to train your "ear memory."

E *E*ngrave the word. Write it slowly and firmly so that your hand becomes familiar with the feel of writing it. This is your "muscle memory."

L *L*ook for a

L *L*ink, a mnemonic device or some other unique aspect of the spelling that will fix the word in your "association memory."

Try the SPELL method with *inoculate,* a word from the preceding list.

S Stare at the word m "i-n-o-c-u-l-a-t-e." Notice that there are no double consonants. People who misspell the word usually do so by adding an extra *n*.

P Pronounce the word by exaggerating the syllables: IN-OC-U-LATE.

E Engrave the word: _____.
Write it slowly and firmly. Engrave the word again: _____. Sense in the muscles of your hand how it feels to write the word.

L Look for a

L Link. If you look in the dictionary, you will see that this is the only word (along with its other forms) that

begins with the letters *inoc.* Always associate this
word with its very unique beginning.

Take some time now to apply the SPELL technique to some
words from the "most frequently misspelled" word list.

Exercise 7.9

In this exercise the correct spellings of twenty words from
the "most frequently misspelled" word list are paired with
their most common misspellings. Underline the correct spelling of each word. Check your answers.

1. accordian, accordion
2. annialate, annihilate
3. commitment, committment
4. commitee, committee
5. consensus, concensus
6. desparate, desperate
7. ecstasy, ecstacy
8. harass, harrass
9. ideosyncracy, idiosyncrasy
10. quandary, quandry
11. saxaphone, saxophone
12. stratagem, strategem
13. superintendant, superintendent
14. liason, liaison
15. inoculate, innoculate
16. mischevious, mischievous

17. permissible, permissable
18. incalcuable, incalculable
19. hypocrisy, hypocracy
20. geurilla, guerrilla

Exercise 7.10

Underline the correctly spelled word in the pairs listed below.

1. incidentally, incidently
2. indispensable, indispensible
3. inocuous, innocuous
4. irresistable, irresistible
5. occurrence, occurrance

6. preceed, precede
7. rythm, rhythm
8. analyse, analyze
9. buereau, bureau
10. descendant, decendant

7.6 Outlaws with Special Diacritical Marks

Many words have been absorbed so recently into English from French, Spanish, German, Portuguese, and Italian that they still retain diacritical marks, that is, symbols for pronunciation. Most of these words, like *céleste,* you will rarely use, but some are common. The alternate word for restaurant, strictly speaking, should have an accent mark over its final letter, *café.* Your writing professor may have found one of your expressions old, worn out, trite, and marked it *cliché.* If so, you and he or she know how the word is spelled properly. Eventually such words will pass completely into English and drop the marks, but until then, you might as well be careful and reap the credit for being astute.

façade: meaning the face, or front, often used in architecture (The mark is called a cedilla.)

Voilà!: meaning "there it is!" or "I have it!"

céleste: a stop on an organ

dénouement: the clarification or solution of the plot of a play or story

crème de la crème: the cream of the cream, the very best, the most choice

première: the opening or first night of a show; the leading woman dancer

Pietá: any representation, usually a painting or sculpture, of Mary holding the dead Jesus

après ski: the party or gathering after skiing

Some proper names often are treated as if they were being spelled in the native language, for instance, Søren Kierkegaard.

This discussion will not show you all words that have special markings. Its purpose is to encourage you, as you absorb words into your vocabulary, to be more sensitive than the average writer is about special treatment of words. We certainly do not suggest that you adopt ostentatious, snobbish, show-off spellings. We have already suggested that you avoid the British spellings *colour, harbour, armour, humour, kerb,* and *tyre;* you should use their American forms: *color, harbor, armor, humor, curb,* and *tire.* In fact, if you use a direct quotation from a British book and therefore retain the British spelling, you might wish to add an editor's "*[sic]*," meaning "thus," or "I found it this way in the quotation." If you come across any misspellings or factual errors in a quote, you should insert the "*[sic]*" and let your source take the blame for the mistake.

Now test your knowledge. You have practiced the S-P-E-L-L "spelling fix" by seeing the words, writing them carefully while

Better Spelling

concentrating on sight and feel, and using mnemonic devices for each.

Exercise 7.11

Proofread the paragraph for misspelled outlaws, writing the correct spelling for any error in the blank provided. Check your answers.

1. _____ Athletes almost allways have a lot of

2. _____ insentive to stay in shape until the

3. _____ season ends. Weather or not they keep

4. _____ up an exersize program after the season

5. _____ ends depends on their attitudes toward

6. _____ themselves as "total athletes." Alot of

7. _____ planning goes into their physical fitness

8. _____ programs for the off-season while they are

9. _____ still in the midst of the schedule.

10. _____ Therefor, they are always

11. _____ delt quite a blow when they find that they

12. _____ must forego the training table for the

13. _____ menue of the local diner when the

14. _____ season ends. Although less than good

15. _____ food does not necessarily imply a trip

16. _____ to the cemetary, total athletes

17. _____ expect more then just to fill their bellies.

●●

7.7 Summary

●●

A. Outlaws are words that appear to have arbitrary or illogical spellings. Actually every word has a more or less traceable history, as we learn in the study of etymology, so no spelling is purely arbitrary. In some cases, such as the word *ghost,* the bothersome letter (*h* in *ghost*) is a carryover from an earlier pronunciation.

B. Mnemonic devices—little rhymes or sayings that remind you of thd correct spelling of a word—are particularly helpful with outlaw words. The saying "you get to the cemetery with ease (*e's!*)" is a mnemonic device, since it helps you to remember that there are three *e's* in *cemetery.*

C. It is important to use the spelling fix, a concentrated effort of the ear, hand, and eye muscles, on outlaw words in order to retain their correct spellings in your memory.

D. The dictionary is your best reference source for spelling. Always look up an outlaw word if you are uncertain of its spelling.

E. You should keep a "most wanted" list of your own pet outlaws, those that constantly give you trouble.

F. Only one word, *supersede,* ends in *sede.* Only three words, *exceed, proceed,* and *succeed,* end in *ceed.* All the rest of the words that end in that sound are spelled with *cede.*

Exercise 7.12

Underline the correct spelling of the words in the parentheses below. Answers are at the back of the book.

Example: There is iron in this mountain (enviroment, <u>environment</u>).

1. (Procede, Proceed) to the stop light and turn left.

2. The rebellious states (seceded, seceeded) from the union.

Better Spelling

3. It is essential to (develope, develop) a fine ear if your intonation is going to be correct.

4. To his dismay he was (dealt, delt) three aces in the first hand.

5. Your (exercise, exersize) program must be curtailed or you'll reinjure your knee.

6. They had to wait (untill, until) the last bus had left the station before closing.

7. It is (therefor, therefore) impossible to grant a leave of absence at this time.

8. It doesn't matter (whether, weather) the envelope is sealed or not.

9. You may keep your (menue, menu) as a souvenir.

10. She had (allready, already) submitted her application to the department.

Chapter 8
Finishing Touches

8.1 Key Words in College Papers

Business people are most annoyed at the misspelling of names, places, and products. In college papers the misspellings that cause the most distress (besides the name of the course and of the professor) are those of key terms. Imagine what a professor thinks of a paper whose intent is to demonstrate an understanding of existentialism—and the word itself is misspelled in the title and throughout the paper. "How can he understand it when he can't even spell it?" is the instructor's illogical but certainly understandable and inevitable reaction. Students work so hard on their papers that they sometimes find the last-minute editing and proofreading almost impossible; even so, they should make a final effort to check that all the important words are spelled correctly. When you proofread, you may habitually start with the text of the theme, but do not forget that what your instructor sees first and most impressionably is the title.

In the following columns you will find words that are important in various fields. Look through the list, see which ones you will particularly need, and make sure that you know how

Better Spelling

to spell them. By now you may be tired of our reminder that you must exercise all your sense memories, but the advice still holds. Robert Montgomery, an authority on memory training, comments that 85 percent of what we learn and remember comes through our eyes, 11 percent through our ears, and 3 or 4 percent through our taste, touch, or smell; but most studies indicate that it is impossible to isolate how we learn to spell. Using all the senses to buttress each other seems to be what works best. As you look at a word that you wish to remember, stare at it, close your eyes and see the word; sound it out syllable by syllable, perhaps artificially accenting or emphasizing a letter (math-E-matics, an-al-Y-sis, ex-is-tEn-Tial-ism, Re-naiS-Sance); then mentally or actually write the word out. *See* it in your penmanship.

Sciences:	dimension	protein
absorption	ellipse	quadrant
alkaline	empirical	salivary
ambivalence	enzyme	soluble
analogy	equation	sulfur
analysis	exponents	symmetric
antibiotic	fission	theorem
binomial	fusion	**Social Sciences:**
botanical	gestation	accrual
catalyst	glucose	anarchy
cellulose	hybrid	annual
chlorophyll	hydrochloric	behavior
coefficient	inoculate	behaviorism
data, datum	integral	beneficiary
determinant	proportion	bureaucracy

cognitive	oligarchy	hedonism
communication	personnel	humanism
conglomerate	plutocracy	iambic pentameter
counselor	preemptive	impressionism
crisis	residence	metaphysics
depreciation	sovereign	onomatopoeia
differential	**Humanities:**	parallel
dissension	achromatic	percussion
egocentrism	acoustic	plagiarism
electoral	aesthetic	platonic
fiscal	antithesis	protagonist
government	architecture	rhythm
gubernatorial	bass	sequel
indicator	chiaroscuro	soliloquy
intangible	clef	symbolism, symbol
irrational	column	temperament
mechanism	dynamics	villain
monarchy	elision	
monopolistic	ethics	
negotiable	genre	

Exercise 8.1

In the following exercise, proofread for misspellings these sentences taken from college essays. Put the correct spellings

Better Spelling

in the blanks at the end of the sentences. Check your answers before proceeding.

1. The material is noted for its absorbtion of liquids.

   _____

2. The buraucracy was unable to recognize the problems of the individual citizen. _____

3. The tribe's architeture was primitive but graceful.

   _____

4. The experiments were conducted in the botanacal gardens of the university. _____

5. Piaget is noted for his theory of cognative development.

   _____

6. The collumns were immense and perfectly symmetrical.

   _____

7. An ellips can be formed from a conic section.

   _____

8. The adjective phrases must be paralell in form.

   _____

9. The sovreign rights of the individual were threatened by the revolution. _____

10. The rythm of the poem is perfectly consistent through the first 10 lines. _____

Exercise 8.2

Here are 20 more terms frequently used in college papers. Underline the correct spelling in each pair of terms. Check your answers.

1. alkalyne, alkaline
2. ambivelance, ambivalence
3. analogy, alanogy
4. antebiotic, antibiotic
5. binomial, binomiel
6. catalyst, catalist
7. celulose, cellulose
8. chloraphyl, chlorophyll
9. annual, annuel
10. beneficiary, benificiary
11. contingent, contingant
12. counsellor, counselor
13. crisis, crissis
14. depreciation, depreciacion
15. dominence, dominance
16. ethicks, ethics
17. sequel, sequell
18. symbolism, symbalism
19. temprament, temperament
20. villian, villain

8.2 Spelling Errors That Really Hurt

Please read this letter:

Dear Matt:

Since you used to have an uncle who was a lawyer you may be smart. Besides you are an old friend. I got to have help. Tell me what to do. My husband Dan wants to be a sailor again and to hang around the piano at the USO showing off his new uniform. It is getting monopolis listening to his talk. He says he will make more money. When I try to talk sense, he says, "keep your mouth shut you old battlewagon." He even thinks I am a boat. I don't like his attitue. I got no gredients against the navy, but I don't think he can be a sailor again because he has syracuse veins and both legs are shorter than the other. That's my sediments anyhow. When I was sick in bed last month with all the heat and humility, he kept singing "Ankles Away" and throwing salt water all over the house. Do I have to let him be a sailor again? He acts a little bomby and gave me a woman's form to fill out with 2 wetnesses. Give me some dope. I am a fiscal wreck. Hope you are the same.

Louise

This tragic letter makes people laugh. It, or similar letters, keep appearing in humor magazines. Why is it funny? Because humor is often cruel; people laugh with relief to find that "someone else" can make mistakes.

Throughout this book we have tried to remind you that there are many reasons for you to spell accurately and carefully. Very often we have had students ask "What does it matter if I am a poor speller? You can tell what I mean." In the first place that is often not true. A misspelled word often causes confusion; it makes a reader puzzle as to the meaning of a sentence. A misspelling, moreover, always causes a reader to judge the writer. Confronting the misspelling, the reader almost always thinks one, part, or all of these:

"What a careless guy . . . He must not think this letter is important. He didn't even bother to go back over it and correct the spelling of a three-letter word."

"He must not be very smart; he can't even spell *too.*"

"Wow! The schools today must be awful. This kid can't spell anything."

This attitude (the letter writer at the beginning of this section spelled it "attitue") is not limited to teachers. If anything, it is less common among teachers—who are trained to consider writing for its ideas and information as well as for its spelling. Having worked in industry, in the military, in politics, in civic activities, and in the field of art and culture, we have seen uncounted letters that have circles around misspellings and unkind comments about the letter writers.

What we want to emphasize here is that some misspellings are worse than others. If the misspellings are so serious that they make your reader question your abilities, you are in real trouble. The purpose of this section of the book is to help you avoid that kind of error.

Start out by looking back at the letter from Louise to old friend Matt. What are the misspellings? What did poor Louise really mean?

---

monopolis should be *monotonous*
attitue should be *attitude*
gredients should be *grievance*
syracuse should be *varicose*
sediments should be *sentiments*
humility should be *humidity*
Ankles should be *Anchors*
bomby should be *balmy*
wetnesses should be *witnesses*
fiscal means "financial"; Louise probably means *physical*

145

Exercise 8.3

Underline the correct spelling in each of the parentheses below. Check your answers.

1. The exam was (monopolis, monotonous).

2. She had a negative (attitude, attitue).

3. The union filed a (grievance, gredients).

4. (Syracuse, Varicose) veins can be treated medically.

5. My (sentiments, sediments) are not to favor the proposal.

6. The (humility, humidity) is high today.

7. The (ankles, anchors) of the ship were raised.

8. The weather in Florida is often (bomby, balmy).

9. His doctor gives him a (fiscal, physical) test every year.

10. There were two (witnesses, wetnesses) to the crime.

Here are some misspellings that really cause the reader to stop in the middle of a sentence. Look for the errors as you read the sentences. An explanation of the error is given below each sentence.

Our football team never was underfeeted.

undefeated (Funny because it suggests the poor team was underfoot.)

At a university the president is the most important clog in the machine.

Horrors! A *clog* gets in the way—a *cog* helps.

In reply to your lust letter...

---

last letter!

In our 4-H club we took turns being head of the working crew. We worked in the barn when I was the manger.

---

manager

I was born in a suburp of San Jose.

---

suburb

One woman in our department possesses unhounded energy.

---

unbounded

I was born in a navel reservation.

---

naval, meaning related to the navy; *navel* refers to the center of the stomach.

147

Better Spelling

When taking notes, avoid taking down the professor's speech in its eternity.

---

entirety

What the book shows is that man needs a higher archy to help him.

---

hierarchy

He must watch his waste if he eats too much.

Yuk! *waist*

My room at home has a beautiful old chester drawers.

---

chest of drawers

My father likes foreign hand ties. I like beau ties.

---

four-in-hand; bow ties

After I had garnished enough evidence, I made my decision.

Garnished means "decorated." *Garnered* means "gathered."

He did not play that day, and for all intensive purposes he could have stayed at home that day.

---

intents and purposes

He is a man of many faucets.

You know what a faucet is; *facet* means "sides" or "dimensions."

Because of many troubles she felt she had to flea her country.

Flea is an insect; the word is *flee*.

I enjoyed the senator's speech, but it made me sad. I was lost in a veil of tears.

The expression should be *vale of tears*. *Vale* means "valley"; a *veil* covers a bride's face.

Exercise 8.4

Underline the correct spelling within the parentheses in each sentence. Check your answers.

1. The team was (underfeated, undefeated).

2. The bone will (cog, clog) the drain.

3. The feeling of (last, lust) is very powerful.

4. She has (unfounded, unbounded) love for her faithful husband.

5. The lecture seemed to last for an (eternity, entirety).

6. This (chester drawers, chest of drawers) is an antique.

7. The lawyer (garnered, garnished) convincing evidence.

8. She had to (flee, flea) from the approaching flood.

9. The professor has started to wear (beau, bow) ties.

10. Have you ever worn a (foreign hand, four-in-hand) tie?

•••

8.3 Correct Spellings That Really Impress People

•••

Do any of these items in recent magazines or newspapers do anything for you?

In a metropolitan newspaper there was the headline "The Media Is Blamed for Poor Reading Habits." *Media* is plural. It should be "The Media Are . . ."

An advertisement in *The Rocky Mountain News:* "Tom Boy Clothes Are Alright!" In the cartoon "The Amazing Spiderman," a hospital orderly asks, "Are you alright, sir?" There is no such word as *alright* in English. It should be *all right.*

Another headline: "Criteria Is Changed To Evaluate Recession." *Criteria* is plural. It should be *Criterion.*

What we hoped you noticed is that even professional writers and editors can make spelling errors. We reason here that if you can spell words commonly misspelled in magazines, newspapers, and books, and in the correspondence of people who should know better, then you will indeed impress your readers when you present a letter or paper with the demons properly spelled.

In over five hundred letters of application written by prospective teachers of college English, most of whom had Ph.D.'s, only seventeen of them had the word *résumé* spelled correctly at the top of their credentials! Apparently not many people know that both of the *e*'s should have marks over them, called the acute accent. Those who did not call the information the *résumé* had another name for it—and often misspelled it— *curriculum vitae.* Knowing just a little Latin but not enough, some writers call it *curriculum vita,* which is a singular form for the second word. What is required is a possessive, which explains why it should be *curriculum vitae.* You can imagine what the search committee thought of English teachers who had misspellings in so important a letter. You can also see that if you get the words right, you will be off to a head start.

Exercise 8.5

Underline the correct spellings in the parentheses. Check your answers.

1. The waiter asked, "Is everything (all right, alright)?"

2. Yearly income is not the only (criteria, criterion) for success in business.

3. It is essential to submit a (resumé, résumé) with each application form.

4. When you apply for a faculty position, you must include a copy of your curriculum (vita, vitae).

5. The news (media, medium) was cleared of all charges by the jury.

151

Remember that *criterion* and *medium* are singular nouns; the plural forms are *criteria* and *media*. *Résumé* has diacritical marks over both *e*'s. Don't forget the *e* in *curriculum vitae*, and don't ever use the word *alright*. You must say *all right*.

• •

8.4 Spelling Proper Nouns

• •

Moving up the scale from worst mistakes to the still very bad, we should consider the kinds of mistakes that too often assail the eyes of a college admissions officer or of a personnel director reading letters of application. Some students who might have been admitted to a college were not because they misspelled the name of the college. Some applicants just might have received a job—had they not misspelled the name of the company. Hundreds of letters fail in their purpose because they contain a misspelling of the name of the person addressed.

As you read letters you receive from friends and associates you should get into the habit of fixing on the spelling of proper nouns, the capitalized names of people and companies, products and processes. As you read letters realize that eventually you will want to answer them, and the easiest way to write a poor and ineffective letter is to misspell some of those names. Put the spelling fix on names and places. Is it Smith or Smythe? Is it Stephen or Steven, Jeffrey or Geoffrey, Debby or Debbie, McLellan or McClellan, Snyder or Schneider? Is it McDonald, MacDonald, or McDonnell? Alice or Alyce? Is it Jablonski or Jablonsky? A man named Henry Tacedelowski once said that he liked anyone who spelled his name correctly. Think how Carl Yastrzemski and Aleksandr Solzhenitsyn must feel about their names. A famous pianist with a difficult name to spell once gave an anthologist permission to use one of his essays in a collection; but when the anthologist sent a letter of appreciation with the name misspelled, the pianist sent the letter back in a rage and rescinded permission for the article, costing the publisher and editors a great deal of money.

The best advice is for you to keep all your important correspondence and check the spelling of all names.

Exercise 8.6

Here is a list of the names of prominent American political figures. The names have appeared many thousands of times in print. You are very likely familiar with all of the names, but can you spell them correctly? Correct the misspellings, writing your corrections in the blanks beside the names. Check your answers.

1. Linden Johnson   _____

2. John F. Kennedey   _____

3. George Busch   _____

4. Eleanor Rosevelt   _____

5. Abraham Lincon   _____

6. Dwight D. Eisenhauer   _____

7. Thomas Jefersson   _____

8. John Quincy Addams   _____

9. Martin Luthor King, Jr.   _____

10. Nelson Rockerfeller   _____

Don't be too concerned if you made some mistakes. The point here is that many people misspell names they know *by sound* very well. When you write, be sure that you proofread carefully for the spelling of names.

Exercise 8.7

Now look at the following list of college courses. You have seen and heard these or similar course titles before. Can you spot the misspellings on the list? Write corrections in the blanks beside each title.

1. Europeon History _____

2. Introductary Spannish _____

3. American Civilisation _____

4. Latan American Studys _____

5. Advansed Phisycs _____

6. Asion Culturel History _____

7. Popular Modren Novals _____

8. English as a Foriegn Languadge _____

9. Introdution to Philosaphy _____

10. Marketting and Managment _____

8.5 Spelling Place Names

Place names frequently give trouble, including the ones in the following list, chosen because they contain tricky and potentially troublesome letter combinations. Note any special diacritical marks. Some pronunciations are included; note how some sounds are formed differently.

Aberdeen (Scotland)

Appleton (Wisconsin)

Ardmore (Pennsylvania)

Bergen (Norway)

Bethesda (Maryland)

Boca Raton (Florida)

Calais (Maine and France)

Cameroon (Africa)

Córdoba (Spain, Mexico)

Cordova (United States)

Czechoslovakia

Dobbs Ferry (New York)

Duquesne (pronounced "doo-kane")

Elmira (New York)

Elmhurst (Illinois)

Eudora

Gila (pronounced "heel-a")

Guadalupe (Spain, Mexico, United States)

Guadeloupe (France, West Indies)

Hawaii

Hiroshima (Japan)

Ivory Coast (Africa)

Juárez (Mexico)

Juneau (Alaska)

Kankakee (Illinois)

Khyber Pass (Pakistan)

La Jolla (pronounced "la hoya," California)

Lakeview (in 10 states)

Lake View (in five states)

Londonderry (New Hampshire)

Madagascar (Africa)

Madras (India)

Maritime Provinces (Canada)

Melbourne (Australia)

Monterey (California)

Monterrey (Mexico)

Nez Perce (Idaho)

Nezperce (also in Idaho)

Northwest Cape

North West Providence

North-West Frontier (Pakistan)

Oldford (Tennessee)

Old Fort (Texas)

Better Spelling

Oslo (Norway)

Oroville (California)

Orrville (in three states)

Poughkeepsie (New York)

Port O'Connor (Texas)

Puerto Rico

Qatar (Pakistan)

Quebec (Canada)

Rabbithash (Kentucky)

Rabbit Ears (Colorado)

Redcliff (in two states)

Red Cliff (Wisconsin)

Red Cliffe (in two states)

Rocky Ford (in two states)

Rockyford (South Dakota)

Saint Louis (Missouri)

Saint-Luc (Quebec)

Schenectady (New York)

Shelburne (Vermont)

Stephan (South Dakota)

Stephen or Stephens (in many states)

Stevens (in six states)

Three Mile Island (Pennsylvania) *but*

Twentynine Palms (California)

Vaidés (Argentina)

Valdez (pronounced "val-dez" in Colorado *but* "val-deez" in Alaska)

Valencia (Pennsylvania and Spain)

Valentia (Ireland)

Valverda (Louisiana)

Val Verde (Texas)

Washington (99 towns, cities, counties, or states in the United States)

Waverley (in seven states)

Waverly (in three states)

Woodberry (New Jersey) *but*

Middlebury (Connecticut)

Yankee Lake (Ohio) *but*

Yankeetown (Florida, Indiana)

Zeeland (Michigan, North Dakota) *but*

New Zealand

Exercise 8.8

Now for a quiz on the spelling of place names. Proofread the following sentences for spelling errors. Put the correct spelling for each sentence containing an error in the blank provided. Check your answers.

1. Honolulu is the largest city in Hawiai._____

2. The capital of Checkoslovakia was Prague._____

3. French is the first language of the Province of Quebec.

   _____

4. Pittsburgh, Pennsylvania, is known for its industry.

   _____

5. The Martime Provinces are in eastern Canada.

   _____

6. Puorto Rico provides much of the sugar consumed in the United States.

   _____

7. The University of Texas is in Austin._____

8. St. Luois, Missouri, produced many famous jazz musicians.

   _____

9. Monteray, California, is south of San Francisco.

   _____

10. Connecticut is a New England state. _____

● ●

8.6 Keeping Up with New Spellings and Abbreviations

● ●

The really good speller, the one who gets a reputation for care in writing, is one who keeps up on new words. For example, in the United States we are now more frequently encountering the metric system for weights and measures; therefore, we must know a number of new spellings. The following lists common metric terms and their abbreviations:

millimeter	mm	milligram	mg	milliliter	ml
centimeter	cm	centigram	cg	centiliter	cl
decimeter	dm	decigram	dg	deciliter	dl
meter	m	gram	g	liter	L
dekameter	dam	dekagram	dag	dekaliter	dal
hectometer	hm	hectogram	hg	hectoliter	hl
kilometer	km	kilogram	kg	kiloliter	kl

Here's how the system works:

Measurement
A *meter* is a measurement of length.
A *gram* is a measurement of weight.
A *liter* is a measurement of volume.

Amounts
milli = one thousandth (1/1,000)
centi = one hundredth (1/100)
deci = one tenth (1/10)
deka = ten (10)
hecto = one hundred (100)
kilo = one thousand (1,000)

Exercise 8.9

Now check your ability to spell these terms from the metric system. Underline the correct spelling for each pair of words below. Check your answers.

1. millimeter, milimeter
2. centemeter, centimeter
3. desigram, decigram
4. kiloliter, killoliter
5. killagram, kilogram

6. centoliter, centiliter
7. deciliter, decileter
8. hectometer, hectameter
9. kilometer, kilomiter
10. deckagram, dekagram

* *

8.7 A Note on Variant Spellings
* *

After studying the spelling rules, the exceptions to the rules, phonics, outlaws, and some etymology, can we now assume that there is one correct spelling for each word? Almost—but not quite. There are some words in our language that have what are known as variant spellings. This means that such a word may be spelled correctly more than one way. Here are some examples with both currently accepted spellings:

afterward—afterwards
among—amongst (but this is "stiff")
blond—blonde
traveled—travelled
hiccup—hiccough
Pygmy—Pigmy
wisteria—wistaria

Don't worry, there are not many words that have variant spellings, and you can always be sure you are "right" by *using the first spelling listed in the dictionary.*

Remember that spelling in England and America still differs in some cases: *harbour, harbor; colour, color; candour, candor; favour, favor; henour, honor; labour, labor; rumour, rumor; vigour, vigor;* and *kerb, curb.* In most cases it is thought pretentious for Americans to use the British spelling, and the American spelling is therefore preferred.

8.8 Summary

A. Be especially careful of your spelling when you write letters. Spell correctly the names of the addressees, institutions, businesses, and organizations; otherwise, your letter will be given little consideration.

B. On college papers be sure that you spell the names of your instructors correctly. Also use the correct spelling of the courses they teach. Remember that the title page is the first impression of your work. Also be sure to spell correctly the special terminology that you use in each academic area.

C. Remember that good spelling can be impressive. If you correctly spell words that even professional writers misspell, you will influence your reader in a very positive way.

D. Keep up with new spellings as they come into the language.

E. There are some words in our language that have variant spellings. You are always going to be safe by using the first spelling listed in the dictionary.

Exercise 8.10

Proofread the following sentences. Underline the correct spelling in the parentheses. When you are finished, check your results with the answers at the back of the book.

Example: The ambassador had to (flea, <u>flee</u>) the country.

1. The (navel, naval) officers met on the bridge of the ship.

2. The (absorbtion, absorption) of water is what caused the cracks to appear.

3. There should be a double (collumn, column) on the left side of the page.

4. He was falsely accused of (plagarism, plagiarism).

5. There are forty students in the (litterature, literature) class.

6. She has just published her nineteenth article on (botanacal, botanical) studies.

7. He has shown the student how to replace the defective (equasion, equation).

8. One (criteria, criterion) for grading final exams is mechanics.

9. The interview will be based upon your (résumé, resume).

10. You need to see the (sequell, sequel) before you can criticize it fairly and accurately.

Answer Key

Chapter 1 Answer Key

Exercise 1.5
1. companies
2. received
3. than
4. environment
5. tragedy
6. Today's
7. A lot
8. really
9. shining
10. among

Exercise 1.6
1. probably
2. lose
3. forty
4. roommate
5. Their

6. grammar
7. similar
8. definitely
9. realize
10. making

Chapter 2 Answer Key

Exercise 2.1
1. no error
2. competitive, transportation
3. professional, athletes
4. mathematics, different
5. no error
6. interpretation
7. difference
8. definitely
9. pleasant, probably
10. dignity

Spelling Skills

11. no error
12. no error
13. magazines, recognition
14. no error
15. no error
16. anxieties, determining
17. no error
18. no error
19. emphasis
20. academic, environment
21. government
22. no error
23. substitute

Exercise 2.2
1. athlete
2. transportation
3. interpretation
4. mathematics
5. pleasant
6. recognition
7. probably
8. determining
9. emphasis
10. magazines
11. professional
12. anxieties
13. different
14. definitely
15. dignity
16. competitive
17. academic
18. environment

19. government
20. substitute

Exercise 2.3
1. actually
2. different
3. artificial
4. government
5. athlete
6. competition
7. embarrassed
8. photograph
9. relatively
10. pleasant, magazine
11. compliment
12. no error
13. a lot
14. first
15. daily
16. all right
17. their
18. no error
19. suburban
20. just
21. steak
22. police
23. too
24. no error
25. begins

Exercise 2.4
1. vacuum
2. sophomore

3. Separate
4. all right
5. tried
6. athletes
7. transportation
8. government
9. Vengeance
10. suburban

Chapter 3 Answer Key

Exercise 3.1
1. height
2. no error
3. briefcase
4. no error
5. receive
6. achieve
7. no error
8. yielding
9. no error
10. no error
11. relief
12. receipts
13. neighbor
14. weighing
15. no error
16. besieged
17. no error
18. no error
19. chief

Exercise 3.2
1. piece
2. believe
3. receiver
4. field
5. conceive
6. leisure
7. ceiling
8. mischief
9. conceited
10. Neither

Exercise 3.3
1. ceiling
2. weights
3. receipt
4. thief
5. neighboring
6. weighed
7. deceive
8. freight
9. veil
10. niece

Exercise 3.4
1. seismic
2. sieve
3. height
4. sleight
5. foreign
6. died
7. forfeit
8. pimiento

Spelling Skills

9. surfeit
10. friend

Exercise 3.5
1. fielded
2. neighed
3. perceived
4. priest's
5. Efficiency
6. Either
7. deceitfulness
8. ancient
9. grief
10. field

Exercise 3.6
1. no error
2. totally
3. no error
4. no error
5. compelled
6. entering
7. no error
8. no error
9. drastically
10. no error
11. roommate
12. no error
13. no error
14. transferring
15. no error
16. submitted
17. no error

18. rebelling
19. no error
20. no error
21. no error
22. occurred
23. actually
24. no error
25. no error
26. no error
27. finally
28. no error

Exercise 3.7
1. excellent
2. transmitting
3. planned
4. equipped
5. repellent
6. Winning
7. forgotten
8. lessening
9. quitting
10. reasoning
11. unsweetened
12. heated
13. permitted
14. expelled
15. forbidden
16. rebellion
17. curtailed
18. digital
19. pinned
20. allotted

Exercise 3.8
1. no error
2. ebb
3. sweat
4. poured
5. no error
6. staff
7. arc

Exercise 3.9
1. zinc
2. disc
3. gas
4. guess
5. fleck
6. null
7. clef
8. odd
9. fizz
10. purr

Exercise 3.10
1. panicking
2. trafficking
3. frolicked
4. colicky
5. picnicking
6. picnic
7. ridden
8. frolic
9. media
10. frolicking

Exercise 3.11
1. fitter
2. toper
3. sated
4. topping
5. regretting
6. none
7. McFadden
8. letting
9. mitten
10. city

Exercise 3.12
1. picnic
2. panicking
3. dropping
4. regretted
5. forgetting
6. maddening
7. remitted
8. forgotten
9. babysitter
10. baggage

Exercise 3.13
1. norms
2. societies
3. no error
4. no error
5. no error
6. no error
7. woman
8. no error

9. keys
10. sexes
11. species
12. no error
13. no error
14. themselves
15. no error
16. sociologists
17. no error
18. no error
19. cultures
20. halves
21. no error
22. no error

Exercise 3.14
1. messes
2. latches
3. gashes
4. boxes
5. birches
6. princesses
7. hexes
8. masses
9. switches
10. wishes

Exercise 3.15
1. luxuries
2. economies
3. democracies
4. energies
5. Marys

6. summaries
7. hypocrisies
8. industries
9. revolutionaries
10. Harrys

Exercise 3.16
1. turkeys
2. highways
3. holidays
4. alloys
5. trolleys
6. boys
7. plays
8. attorneys
9. chimneys
10. rays

Exercise 3.17
1. fiefs
2. handkerchiefs
3. roofs
4. reefs
5. beliefs
6. tiffs
7. bluffs
8. skiffs
9. whiffs
10. cliffs

Exercise 3.18
1. lives
2. halves

3. wolves
4. shelves
5. wives
6. knives
7. selves
8. loaves
9. leaves
10. sheaves

Exercise 3.19
1. curios
2. rodeos
3. studios
4. banjos
5. zeros
6. solos
7. sopranos
8. concertos
9. ratios
10. stereos

Exercise 3.20
1. embargoes
2. mosquitoes
3. Negroes
4. tornadoes
5. vetoes

Exercise 3.21
1. studios
2. zeros
3. stereos
4. solos

5. mosquitoes
6. vetoes
7. ratios
8. banjos
9. concertos
10. embargoes

Exercise 3.22
1. cherubim
2. seraphim
3. soliloquies
4. alumni
5. alumnae
6. loci
7. fungi
8. radii
9. data
10. phenomena
11. strata
12. analyses
13. bases
14. oases
15. hypotheses
16. parentheses
17. theses

Exercise 3.23
1. monarchies
2. lackeys
3. leaves
4. roofs
5. moose
6. women

Spelling Skills

7. radios
8. volcanoes
9. theses
10. larvae
11. alumnae
12. stereos
13. vetoes
14. daughters-in-law
15. Oxen
16. loaves
17. beliefs
18. summaries
19. Harrys
20. attorneys

Exercise 3.24
1. norms
2. societies
3. no error
4. no error
5. no error
6. no error
7. woman
8. no error
9. keys
10. sexes
11. species
12. no error
13. no error
14. themselves
15. no error
16. sociologists
17. no error

18. no error
19. cultures
20. halves
21. no error
22. no error

Exercise 3.25
1. thieves
2. monkeys
3. finally
4. height
5. detailing
6. halos
7. receive
8. compelling
9. churches
10. opportunities

Chapter 4 Answer Key

Exercise 4.1
1. Except
2. desert
3. no error
4. your
5. already
6. course
7. than
8. no error
9. lose
10. too
11. no error
12. no error

13. who's
14. no error
15. plains

Exercise 4.2
1. affect
2. altered
3. break
4. capital
5. council
6. formerly
7. It's
8. led
9. minor
10. morale
11. passed
12. piece
13. personal
14. principal
15. quite
16. stationery
17. they're
18. compliments
19. threw
20. too

Exercise 4.3
1. advice
2. isle
3. ally
4. angle
5. bearing
6. born

7. Breathe
8. canvas
9. clothes
10. unconscious

Exercise 4.4
1. device
2. decent
3. dual
4. forty
5. regard
6. holly
7. hopped
8. instants

Exercise 4.5
1. lesson
2. nineteenth
3. presence
4. rites
5. scraped
6. site

Exercise 4.6
1. advise
2. aisle
3. alley
4. devise
5. descent
6. regard
7. holy
8. lessons

Spelling Skills

Exercise 4.7

1. Except
2. desert
3. no error
4. your
5. already
6. course
7. than
8. no error
9. lose
10. too
11. no error
12. no error
13. who's
14. no error
15. plains

Exercise 4.8

1. altar
2. led
3. piece
4. past
5. its

Chapter 5 Answer Key

Exercise 5.1

1. dissatisfied
2. no error
3. no error
4. roommates
5. completely
6. unnecessary

7. no error
8. disservice
9. no error
10. closely
11. no error
12. disappointed
13. no error
14. enrollment
15. Finally
16. no error
17. no error
18. really
19. no error
20. no error
21. no error

Exercise 5.2

1. unneeded
2. prearranged
3. dissatisfied
4. misunderstand
5. reenforce
6. relocate
7. coordinate
8. dismember
9. replace
10. misspell

Exercise 5.3

1. ruing
2. argument
3. duly

4. truly
5. bluish

Exercise 5.4
1. traceable
2. produceable
3. managing
4. effaceable
5. influential

Exercise 5.5
1. propelled
2. careful
3. ritually
4. marriageable
5. reexamine
6. rescuing
7. unneeded
8. fulfillment
9. manageable
10. hurried
11. impress
12. salvageable
13. employer
14. profess
15. confiding
16. manually
17. foraging
18. immaterial
19. stories
20. storeys (British spelling)

Exercise 5.6
1. tasteful
2. resentful
3. although
4. also
5. artful
6. almighty
7. hateful
8. peaceful
9. all one
10. welcome

Exercise 5.7
1. professor's
2. no error
3. no error
4. no error
5. no error
6. no error
7. no error
8. freshmen's
9. no error
10. students'
11. no error
12. no error
13. no error
14. no error
15. theirs
16. everyone's
17. doesn't
18. A's, F's
19. no error
20. no error

Spelling Skills

Exercise 5.8
1. Tom's
2. dog's
3. tower's
4. tree's
5. Marie's

Exercise 5.9
1. mattress'
2. lioness'
3. bus's
4. glass's
5. highness'

Exercise 5.10
1. women's
2. oxen's
3. mice's
4. lice's
5. geese's

Exercise 5.11
1. actors'
2. judges'
3. students'
4. wives'
5. painters'

Exercise 5.12
1. its
2. ours
3. yours
4. theirs
5. whose

Exercise 5.13
1. somebody's
2. someone's
3. everybody's
4. one's
5. everyone's

Exercise 5.14
1. mustn't
2. won't
3. they'll
4. we're
5. it's

Exercise 5.15
1. n'S
2. 85's
3. C's
4. 3.5's
5. d's

Exercise 5.16
1. Jean's
2. Firth's
3. Ann's, Mary's
4. John's, Sam's
5. Peter's

Exercise 5.17

1. professor's
2. no error
3. no error
4. no error
5. no error
6. no error
7. no error
8. freshmen's
9. no error
10. students'
11. no error
12. no error
13. no error
14. no error
15. theirs
16. everyone's
17. doesn't
18. A's, F's
19. no error
20. no error

Exercise 5.18

1. disappointment
2. theirs
3. manageable
4. One's
5. making
6. doesn't
7. running
8. women's
9. happier
10. hostess'

Chapter 6 Answer Key

Exercise 6.1

1. extremely
2. perform
3. disastrous
4. no error
5. convenience
6. no error
7. no error
8. no error
9. accommodate
10. no error
11. occasion
12. no error
13. government
14. Success
15. benefit
16. no error
17. tragedy

Exercise 6.2

1. accurate
2. extremely
3. together
4. possesses
5. tomorrow
6. habit
7. convenience
8. necessity
9. similar
10. occurred

Spelling Skills

Exercise 6.3
1. a-mount
2. busi-ness or bus-i-ness
3. oc-ca-sion
4. suc-cess
5. per-formed
6. de-scribe
7. gov-ern-ment
8. prac-ti-cal
9. ac-quaint
10. pro-fes-sor

Exercise 6.4
1. amount
2. business
3. occasion
4. success
5. performed
6. describe
7. government
8. practical
9. acquaint
10. professor

Exercise 6.5
1. disastrous
2. accommodate
3. dependent
4. relevant
5. benefit
6. irresistible
7. indispensable
8. tragedy

9. inventor
10. jeweler

Exercise 6.6
1. op-por-tu-ni-ty
2. cur-ric-u-lum
3. war-rant
4. a-cross
5. im-age
6. ex-ag-ger-ate
7. sep-a-rate
8. or-dered
9. ex-pla-na-tion
10. com-fort-a-ble

Exercise 6.7
1. opportunity
2. curriculum
3. warrant
4. across
5. image
6. exaggerate
7. separate
8. ordered
9. explanation
10. comfortable

Exercise 6.8
1. extremely
2. perform
3. disastrous
4. no error
5. convenience

6. no error
7. no error
8. no error
9. accommodate
10. no error
11. occasion
12. no error
13. government
14. Success
15. benefit
16. no error
17. tragedy

Exercise 6.9

1. personnel
2. pronunciation
3. accommodate
4. occasion
5. benefit
6. separate
7. exaggerate
8. opportunity
9. tomorrow
10. government

Chapter 7 Answer Key

Exercise 7.1

1. incentive
2. until
3. whether
4. precise
5. therefore

6. almost
7. dealt
8. menu
9. already
10. always

Exercise 7.2

1. separate
2. environment
3. knowledge
4. privilege
5. address
6. dilemma
7. desperate
8. ecstasy
9. cemetery
10. prevalent

Exercise 7.3

1. anesthetize
2. surprise
3. advertise
4. memorize
5. compromise
6. exercise
7. sensitize
8. supervise
9. revise
10. dependent
11. acre
12. massacre
13. attendant
14. defendant

15. inquire
16. insure
17. repentant
18. lucre
19. baptize
20. disguise

Exercise 7.4

1. precede
2. exceed
3. secede
4. recede
5. supersede
6. cede
7. proceed
8. concede
9. succeed
10. intercede

Exercise 7.5

1. *g*
2. *k*
3. *P*
4. *w,t*
5. *m*
6. *p,e*
7. *p,l*
8. *p,e*
9. *n*
10. *w*
11. *gh*
12. *gh*
13. *n*
14. *n*

Exercise 7.6

1. *c*
2. *h*
3. *w*
4. *h*
5. *g*
6. *p*
7. *n*
8. *w,gh*
9. *w*
10. *h*
11. *h*
12. *h*
13. *w*
14. *g*
15. *c*
16. *h*
17. *h*
18. *b*

Exercise 7.7

1. k
2. w
3. m
4. w
5. gh
6. n
7. n
8. h
9. b
10. P

Exercise 7.8
1. awe inspiring
2. first-rate
3. hung
4. accommodate
5. manner

Exercise 7.9
1. accordion
2. annihilate
3. commitment
4. committee
5. consensus
6. desperate
7. ecstasy
8. harass
9. idiosyncrasy
10. quandary
11. saxophone
12. stratagem
13. superintendent
14. liaison
15. inoculate
16. mischievous
17. permissible
18. incalculable
19. hypocrisy
20. guerrilla

Exercise 7.10
1. incidentally
2. indispensable
3. innocuous

4. irresistible
5. occurrence
6. precede
7. rhythm
8. analyze
9. bureau
10. descendant

Exercise 7.11
1. always
2. incentive
3. Whether
4. exercise
5. no error
6. A lot
7. no error
8. no error
9. no error
10. Therefore
11. dealt
12. no error
13. menu
14. no error
15. no error
16. cemetery
17. than

Exercise 7.12
1. Proceed
2. seceded
3. develop
4. dealt
5. exercise

6. until
7. therefore
8. whether
9. menu
10. already

Chapter 8 Answer Key

Exercise 8.1
1. absorption
2. bureaucracy
3. architecture
4. botanical
5. cognitive
6. columns
7. ellipse
8. parallel
9. sovereign
10. rhythm

Exercise 8.2
1. alkaline
2. ambivalence
3. analogy
4. antibiotic
5. binomial
6. catalyst
7. cellulose
8. chlorophyll
9. annual
10. beneficiary
11. contingent
12. counselor

13. crisis
14. depreciation
15. dominance
16. ethics
17. sequel
18. symbolism
19. temperament
20. villain

Exercise 8.3
1. monotonous
2. attitude
3. grievance
4. Varicose
5. sentiments
6. humidity
7. anchors
8. balmy
9. physical
10. witnesses

Exercise 8.4
1. undefeated
2. clog
3. lust
4. unbounded
5. eternity
6. chest of drawers
7. garnered
8. flee
9. bow
10. four-in-hand

Answer Key

Exercise 8.5
1. all right
2. criterion
3. résumé
4. vitae
5. medium

Exercise 8.6
1. Lyndon
2. Kennedy
3. Bush
4. Roosevelt
5. Lincoln
6. Eisenhower
7. Jefferson
8. Adams
9. Luther
10. Rockefeller

Exercise 8.7
1. European History
2. Introductory Spanish
3. Civilization
4. Latin, Studies
5. Advanced Physics
6. Asian Cultural
7. Modern Novels
8. Foreign Language
9. Introduction, Philosophy
10. Marketing, Management

Exercise 8.8
1. Hawaii

2. Czechoslovakia
3. no error
4. no error
5. Maritime
6. Puerto
7. no error
8. St. Louis
9. Monterey
10. no error

Exercise 8.9
1. millimeter
2. centimeter
3. decigram
4. kiloliter
5. kilogram
6. centiliter
7. deciliter
8. hectometer
9. kilometer
10. dekagram

Exercise 8.10
1. naval
2. absorption
3. column
4. plagiarism
5. literature
6. botanical
7. equation
8. criterion
9. résumé
10. sequel

Index

A

Apostrophes, 97ff

B

British spelling,
    123-124, 160

C

Compound plurals, 64ff
Compound words, 96ff
Consonants, 40ff
Contraction, 102ff
Coordinate nouns, 104f

D

Derivatives, 54ff
Diacritical
    marks, 25-27,134f
Dictionary, 29-32

E

Esoteric words, 128ff
Etymology, 119
Exercises, 5-15, 19-20,
    31-33, 37-38, 40-48,
    51-56, 58-71, 73-74,
    80-81, 85-105, 107-110,
    113-118, 121-122,
    124-127, 130, 133-134,
    136-138, 141-143,
    146-151, 153-154, 157,
    159, 161

F

Final consonants, 46ff
French words, 124f

G

Greek words, 124f